SMOKY DAYS AND SLEEPLESS NIGHTS

A Century or so with the Albion Fire Department

This book is a work of nonfiction. The author aspires to be completely historically accurate, but as with any historical work, some records have been lost or destroyed and educated guesses have to be made. The author indicates in the text when he makes one of these suppositions.

All profits of this book benefit the Albion Volunteer Fire Department. The author grants rights to the AFD to publish, copy, sell, and distribute the book. The author makes no money, tax credit, or other profit from this book; it is his labor of love to the fire department.

For book extras and additional books by the author, please visit:
www.MarkRHunter.com

Published by the Albion Fire Department via CreateSpace
First Edition printing

SMOKY DAYS AND SLEEPLESS NIGHTS:
A Century or so with the Albion Fire Department

By

Mark R. Hunter

THE STORY OF THE STORY

I never meant to write a book.

Well, not this book, anyway. When I realized the Albion Fire Department was approaching its 100th anniversary, I decided to write a short newspaper feature, or maybe a leaflet. Everybody loves a leaflet. I figured a few evenings of research in the library, a few more at the typewriter, then fame and fortune -- or at least fame.

That was a quarter of a century ago.

In a first flurry of activity I spent over 80 hours in research, most of it in front of the microfilm machine at the Noble County Public Library. Weeks more went into two rough drafts and a final manuscript – typed in the old fashioned sense, on an actual typewriter. We're talking the bad old days, before computers and word processing programs. The old, innocent, technology deficient days.

The 80s.

I went through 350 sheets of typing paper (I counted. I have no life.), and began to research carpal tunnel syndrome, just in case.

But of course, nobody asked me to do this: Like the AFD, this project was voluntary. So, after a twenty year sabbatical that most would call real life and raising children, I'm back to see this story through.

I hope that seasoning period will let this final project be less of a dry, dusty tome, and more like something that can be enjoyed even by those who aren't interested in history. After all, I'm no historian: I'm a novelist and humor columnist. While I try to be historically accurate, I've added a little of what some would call my trademark humor, and others would call my trademark lack of the same. If I can make someone smile and keep reading, maybe they'll accidentally learn along the way.

Bob Gagen, Noble County Historian, is the one who uncovered the AFD's official creation date: May 4, 1888. Because of my innocent belief that this would be a small, easy job, I didn't begin to research in earnest until late 1987 – after all, how long could it take to gather enough material for five or ten pages?

Unfortunately, I seldom had the exact dates of historical events. For instance, while trying to find information on the purchase of Albion's 1929 fire engine, I waded through microfilms from newspapers that covered all of 1929. I'd find a short paragraph sandwiched between two dozen other articles under the title "personal paragraphs" or "around town". No headlines, few pictures, lots of small print. I stumbled across interesting material (well, interesting to me), but usually not what I wanted.

Soon I had enough to write a 25 page article, which I asked some of Albion's other firefighters to read. They pointed out mistakes and gave me more information, which often raised even more questions. Did Albion really get by with one hand pumped fire engine for over 40 years? If we had just one, how did we utilize three hose carts? Where did they build the first fire station, and what happened to it? Where did I put the aspirin?

If I'd known how much work would be involved, I might never have started. But I kept on, prodded onward sometimes by my then-wife, who would ask, "Aren't you going to the library tonight?" even though she'd have rather had me at home. I think.

May 4th came and went, and I wasn't ready. Luckily, the fire department's centennial celebration was postponed out of fear it would conflict with the Noble County Courthouse centennial, and then again because we wanted to show off a new fire engine we had on

Albion Fire Chief Larry Huff speaks at the Albion Fire Department's Centennial Celebration, flanked by elected and firefighting officials from across the area.

order.

Eventually we held the celebration, with that short article in a pamphlet. Few people read my story in its entirety. The AFD members discussed publishing it as a fundraiser for the fire department, but the printer's estimate of $800 for just 50 copies stopped us cold. It meant a huge risk, to spend that kind of money with no guarantee of a return. But Print on Demand technology has significantly lowered the cost, so now you hold the final product, with the profits going to the fire department and the credit to me. I can live with that.

Listing every structure fire the AFD ever fought would take a book in itself; listing every call of any kind they answered would take a work the size of an encyclopedia. I eschewed that (it's a real word; look it up), and instead tried to keep the non-firefighter reader awake. Still, I wish I'd spent more time at the library, and interviewed the retired firefighters still living. I'm sure they'd be happy to talk, and I'd be happy to listen; but the formal term "interview", makes me quake in fear. Maybe if I'd thought of it as going to hear war stories, I'd have put more time into it.

If anyone – firefighter or not – reads this and finds a mistake, or has something to add, get in touch with me and I'll take care of it in whatever reprints might come. Or perhaps in the next volume; due to length and time constraints I've ended this story at the century mark, in 1988, and we've already had another quarter century of history since then.

Some details of our distant history I made educated guesses at, using my experience and other events to figure out how the firefighters of the time acted.

Thanks

Of course, no book like this can be written without help. I'm indebted to the *Albion New Era* and *Kendallville News-Sun*, as well as the *Noble County American* and several other newspapers that no longer exist, for much of the information.

I'd also like to thank:

Former Noble County Historian Bob Gagen, who provided the date of the AFD's official establishment and other assistance along the way.

Members of the Albion Fire Department, especially the old timers, for being patient while I pestered them with questions. They also showed interest in my project – firefighters are not renowned for their interest in history, although I've noticed an antique fire truck will get their attention.

The AFD also took a chance and funded the book's printing, despite no guarantee of a return.

The Noble County Public Library, along with the donors and taxpayers who support it. Without the library's historical files, this history would have been impossible. By the time I finished, the librarians just held out the microfilm key as soon as I walked through the door. I began to feel like an expert at solving problems with the microfilm machine.

The Noble County Historical Society and Albion's Old Jail Museum, and all the people of Noble County who see history as more than dry stories in old books.

My wife Emily, who edited this manuscript, formatted it, and designed the cover, as well as giving me the occasionally needed swift kick.

There are others who expressed interest and gave assistance. I'm thankful, because from the time I realized this would be book length, I wondered what in the world I'd do with it when finished. I suppose, like many historians, I can take some comfort in knowing if I hadn't done it, maybe no one would have.

Mark R. Hunter

The author taking photos for the AFD at a live training fire.

THIS BOOK IS DEDICATED TO ALL THE MEN AND WOMEN ACROSS THE WORLD WHO MISS MEALS, SLEEP, WORK, AND FAMILY LIFE TO VOLUNTEER; WHO PUT THEMSELVES IN HARM'S WAY TO FORM A LINE OF DEFENSE AGAINST DISASTER; AND WHO WOULDN'T HAVE IT ANY OTHER WAY. IT'S ESPECIALLY DEDICATED TO THE HUNDREDS OF PEOPLE WHO GAVE THEIR SUPPORT AND SERVICE TO THE ALBION VOLUNTEER FIRE DEPARTMENT OVER THE LAST 125 YEARS.

CHAPTER ONE

Life Without a Fire Department
Or,
Who ya' gonna call?

As with many communities across the country, a series of disastrous fires punctuated Albion's early history. It brought excitement to our little frontier town, which goes to show you – excitement isn't necessarily a good thing.

Being the Noble County Seat didn't spare Albion: In fact, one of the earliest big fires came in 1859 when, not for the first time, Noble County's courthouse burned to the ground.

(The first time happened before the county seat moved to Albion: The courthouse in Augusta, built a few miles west of Albion in 1840, burned in 1843.)

John W. Bryant spotted the fire in Albion's first courthouse at around 1 a.m. on a frigid January morning. He saw flames spread through the clerk's office on the south side of the ground floor, and gave an alarm that likely consisted of a high pitched scream.

In those days, the entire population of a town would turn out to give what help they could at the call of "fire!" In some communities the law stated everyone had to own at least one bucket. As the alarm spread, people would throw their buckets out the window, where they'd be grabbed up, until everyone formed bucket brigades to splash water on the fire.

How many concussions resulted from fallen buckets hasn't been documented.

They splashed water not on the fire but on the neighboring buildings, to prevent a **conflagration** – a big word meaning big fire. When the courthouse burst into flames, many worked to save the other structures on the square – **exposures**, in firefighting terms – while others ran into the burning courthouse to rescue what they could.

When the auditor, treasurer, and recorder showed up to unlock their offices the crowd concentrated on saving important records and papers, along with some furniture. They worked while thick smoke filled the lower floor and fire spread above them, fanned by a strong breeze from the south.

Several people braved the conditions to make their way upstairs. At first they found little fire in the courtroom itself; the fire bypassed that room on its way to the roof.

Then the men spotted a small blaze right above the clerk's office, where oil had been splashed over the floor and wall. Lantern oil? If so, it wasn't where it should be. The burning oil flowed through the cracks to set the first floor Clerk's office on fire, which is where Bryant spotted the flames.

Within fifteen minutes, warning went out that the building's tower threatened to fall through the flame-engulfed attic. Having found important evidence of the fire's cause, those upstairs hurried back down to avoid being crushed or suffocated.

But one man, Hiram T. Tousley, became disoriented. He managed to open a window in the jury room on the north side of the building, then collapsed across the sill while people below him hurried to raise a ladder.

Just as his rescuers got him back down, the tower collapsed through the ceiling into the courtroom and flames engulfed the top floor. Soon after, the courtroom floor also collapsed, which turned the whole building into the 19th Century's biggest tiki torch.

(Tousley recovered, and was on hand to help celebrate eight years later when Hiram S. Tousley – a fellow Albionite, a relative, or possibly the same person – took his oath as Circuit Court Judge. I suspect someone jotted down the wrong initial, in which case Tousley became the first judge to hold that position in the replacement courthouse.)

For others the danger wasn't over that night: The tremendous heat of the blaze carried flaming shingles and pieces of wood half a mile downwind. Although conflagration threatened the entire Courthouse square, especially endangered was the Worden House, a hotel across the street to the northeast – and downwind. Not only did debris rain down on the structure, but waves of radiant heat from the burning courthouse warmed the hotel's roof and siding toward the ignition point.

Albionites formed bucket brigades, then raised ladders and clambered onto the roof with buckets of water for the shingles and walls. In the cold January air, any surface not exposed to the radiated heat iced over, which soon led to tragedy.

George W. Worden was the youngest of three brothers who ran the Worden House. Fortunately, he had one arm around the building's west chimney to support himself, as he dodged embers and splashed water over the roof. When his feet slipped on the ice, he let the chimney support him.

Unfortunately, the chimney couldn't take the weight.

Bricks gave way, and Worden slid down the roof and into the air, to land on his feet twenty feet below.

A group of horrified bystanders carried him into the house, where they discovered both Worden's ankles had been shattered by the impact of the fall. In an exhaustive all-night effort, the people of Albion saved the rest of the town, but they feared the young man would never walk again.

He surprised everyone. Worden not only walked again, but he enlisted in the army, where he served and died in the Civil War five years later.

It seems a miracle no one died that night. In retrospect, it seems a miracle more people haven't been killed or badly injured in the fires that have struck Albion since. In this case, the courthouse burned to the ground, but no other buildings sustained major damage. On other nights Albion wouldn't be so lucky.

A late 1800s photo of Albion looks north, probably from the hill where Albion's first water tower later stood. The town's second courthouse is center left. Just right of center, left of the church steeple that sadly no longer stands, is the Worden House that barely survived the first courthouse fire. (Courtesy Noble County Historical Society)

One fire caused a $20,000 loss. Not much? In the spring of 1867 it was a fortune. Names of owners affected by the single fire include Black, Foster, Leonard, Denny, Prentis, Stephens, Munn, Spencer, Hess, and Baughman. Most of those names appear in Albion phone books to this day, but it took hard work and long hours for them to get back on their financial feet.

Imagine that many buildings leveled in a few hours in your town, and you get the idea.

Once one person's business or house caught fire, the blaze could sweep over other properties and level whole blocks. It happened with some of history's most famous fires, including Chicago, London, and – well, name any great city, and its history includes great conflagrations. Wooden buildings stood close together, and had no sprinkler systems. Often, as with Chicago, even the sidewalks were wood. Half a dozen buildings lost in Albion might not compare to a hundred in New York, but from a relative standpoint it was just as bad.

What about those lucky rural residents, usually farmers, who had no neighbors to be threatened? Small comfort, there – once fire took hold of a home or barn it would take the structure to the ground, and it often took with it outbuildings, livestock, farm equipment, and crops.

One Sunday in 1874, while he was away, the Rev. Jacob Masemore lost his Green Township home southeast of Albion, and all his belongings. The next Tuesday, while in Albion on business, David M. Freeman donated $15 toward a fund to assist the reverend. A short time later, while helpless Albionites watched, a house two miles south of town burned – Freeman's house.

Fire and the County Seat Debate

The danger of fire became an issue in the ongoing debate over the location of the Noble County seat.

Before being made the county seat, Albion was ... nothing. The series of wooded hills became a community only because the people of Noble County voted to make "Center" – the exact center of the county – their capitol. As time went by citizens of Kendallville, and a few from Ligonier, pushed to move the seat to Kendallville, while those in central and southern areas wanted to keep it in Albion. Those in favor of a move searched for any scrap of argument, such as the one reported in the *Albion New Era* in March, 1874:

"There are no vaults for the safekeeping of records at Albion, and if a fire should occur, it would cause great loss."

The *Albion New Era* – as might be expected, considering the name of the publication – leaped to Albion's defense. The editor pointed out that, for a fraction of the cost of relocating the courthouse, fireproof vaults could be built in the present location. But he also claimed that wasn't necessary: "The building is virtually fireproof, and in none of the offices is there wood enough to make a fire sufficient to destroy the record-books. A fire in one office could not communicate with another, and could be extinguished in five minutes."

That sound you hear is all those experienced firefighters slapping their foreheads. Many a "fireproof" building is gutted when fire feeds on furniture and other belongings, called **fire load**. A 1903 fire killed over six hundred people in the all-masonry Iroquois Theater in Chicago, which owners actually *advertised* as "fire proof".

Noble County constructed a new courthouse fourteen years later, anyway. Still, at the time such arguments kept the center of government in Albion.

"Still No Fire Department"

In September, 1875, the cry of "Fire!" once more emptied the courthouse, this time in a different way. Justice Prentiss presided over a trial which, according to the *Albion New Era*, had just "reached that interesting stage when the lawyers were laboring, might and main". The question of whether most people would find arguing lawyers of interest – outside of television – I'll leave for someone else to decide.

Everyone ran to the windows to see smoke rise from the area of Askew & Miller's mills. (Miller had a mill. Heh.) Although the mill lay a few blocks northeast of the Courthouse, the courtroom cleared in record time as spectators and participants rushed to the scene.

They found a wood shed afire on the neighboring property of Charles Haney. Nearby, in danger of being the next victims, a barn full of hay and a home stood. Fast, hard work by the bucket-wielding crowd protected the endangered neighbors, while the shed burned to the ground.

Although citizens managed to keep the flames from spreading – and, it's presumed, the lawyers went back to their mighty, main-y labors – the *Albion New Era* saw problems ahead:

"How much more easily the danger could have been avoided, had there been a few 'hooks and ladders', and an adequate organization, with a supply of regular fire buckets."

This hints Albion didn't pass a "throw out your bucket" ordinance, but relied on any containers, designed for water, milk or whatever, the citizens could find.

"The shed could have been pulled down in two minutes, and all possible danger to surrounding buildings absolutely prevented, with half the labor and excitement. A hook and ladder company, composed of Albion's fire-heroes, would be well-nigh invincible. Why don't we have it?"

Fire-heroes. I like that. The writer, with the word "invincible", showed a lack of knowledge about how hard firefighting can be even with the proper equipment. Still, by asking "Why don't we have it?" he showed he was all too familiar with the danger the town faced.

As if to emphasize the point, just over a week later a lamp exploded in a photograph gallery of A.C. Eagle, in "Clapp's new block". In a small town anything not covered in moss is considered new, but in this case it was accurate: The first brick business block in Albion, the three story Clapp building had been built on the south side of the courthouse square just a few years earlier.

Occupants of the photo gallery quickly smothered the flames. But the near disaster made the point again: If the fire hadn't been doused quickly, as the *Albion New Era* put it, "the entire new block and contiguous buildings would have been consumed. Another appeal for a hook and ladder company."

A quick note on the hook and ladder concept, which we'll examine in more detail later. The idea of attacking a fire head-on didn't even occur to Albion residents: The hook and ladder wagon was a defensive piece of equipment, which carried – wait for it – hooks and ladders. The hooks worked to tear down burning buildings and prevent fire spread.

Again and again fires devastated Albion's business district, where structures stood closest together. In April, 1878, twenty owners suffered losses from a single Sunday morning fire. The *Noble County Democrat* wanted to know: "Shall we have facilities for fighting a fire?"

In June of that year a B&O Railroad elevator burned down. One witness to this fire might have been a man who arrived in Albion to work for the railroad five years before, and who would become Albion's first fire chief; you can assume it made an impression on him.

A month later brought the first advancement in fire protection: a system of cisterns around the courthouse, from which water could be taken to fight fires. It wouldn't have helped the B&O elevator, but it did form a supply of water for defense against flames in the downtown area.

The *Noble County Democrat* suggested local businesses buy hose, but for the time being nothing further happened. Perhaps the editor again showed a certain amount of ignorance about how fires are fought: Cisterns are no more than tanks of water, and without a pump to deliver that water the hose would be useless. The bucket brigade remained the only line of defense.

On Sept 20, 1879, five businesses on South Orange and East Main streets, all two and three story wood frame structures, burned for a $24,000 loss – not adjusted for inflation. (This was on the southeast corner of Albion's main intersection, the geographic center of Noble County and catty-corner from the courthouse, as if cats could be bothered with corners.)

During the fire two kegs of gunpowder exploded, to show that the so-called modern problem of hazardous materials isn't so new, after all. Another fire reportedly razed three buildings at East Hazel and Orange two days later, but old newspaper accounts can be confusing, and it might be the two fires were one and the same. Either way, most of the block disappeared in flames.

Within two weeks, J.D. Black began to raise a new brick building to replace one of those destroyed. To say brick makes for an improvement in the fight against fire spread puts it mildly: This three story structure still stands at the corner of Main and Orange.

Ironically, Albion's second, third, and fourth fire stations all ended up being built in the burned-over space south of the Black building; Albionites know the third as the old Town Hall, and the fourth last held the Albion Police Department before being torn down. The second would have been right between them, but was moved to become an outbuilding at a nearby farm. As far as I can tell no longer exists.

That was all the future, of course. For now, as the *Noble County Democrat* complained in January, 1879 and again in July, 1880: "still no Fire Department".

The fires continued, leveling the post office in July, 1880 (100 years to the month before your friendly author became a firefighter). Brick buildings, although much less likely to spread fire from beyond their contents, offered little safety inside. The 44 by 88 foot Clapp Building was gutted exactly three months after the post office. It had contained, in addition to the previous mentioned Eagle's photo gallery, the Bank of Albion and the Adelphian Dramatic Co. I know nothing of the latter, but that last night became without a doubt their greatest show.

Between 1857 and 1881 over $107,000 – 19th Century dollars, which would be about 2.4 *million* bucks today – worth of property burned. *Not* including the courthouse. Owen Black alone lost $32,000 in a series of blazes that involved his own property. By then, everyone realized water cisterns on the courthouse square offered little protection without an organized fire department to utilize them. Meetings and arguments continued, but still no concrete steps were taken to form one.

8

October 1, 1883: The *Albion New Era's* editor notes "We (Like a newspaperman drinking too much coffee, he used the editorial 'wee') have been a resident of Albion for ten years, and during that period almost the entire business portion of the town has been burned over, and some of it twice."

Those words led an article on the latest conflagration to sweep over the business area, after a few quiet years lulled Albionites into a false sense of security.

This time a row of businesses on the east side of the courthouse square burned, consuming a saloon, barber shop, and bakery/restaurant. Two other buildings – one brick and one with an iron roof – were saved, but badly damaged.

Citizens still filled buckets from the nearest well or cistern and passed them

Albion firefighters make an inside attack during a live fire training session. Mark's camera escaped injury, but his eyebrows will never be the same.

down a line of people, to be thrown on the fire or, more likely, on endangered walls and roofs. If radiant heat forced the bucket brigade away, the property they tried to protect was doomed. The brigade consisted of men who passed full buckets toward the fire, while women and children passed the empty buckets back to the cistern to be refilled. None of them wore any protective clothing, but they had a shot at saving exposures until the fire died down – if those other buildings weren't too close.

The *Albion New Era* commented on the latest fire: "Our people were again strongly impressed with the need of something to battle with the fire fiend."

Maybe so, but after town residents gathered to discuss fire protection at the courthouse in July, 1879, the *Noble County Democrat* termed the meeting a failure.

And yet, 25 years later, the 1908 book "Popular History of Noble County Capitals and Greater Albion" brags: "A paid fire department affords excellent protection." Oh? What made such a huge difference over time?

The changes made over that period, and in years since, saved more homes, businesses, and lives than most people will ever realize.

CHAPTER TWO

Forming a Fire Department
Or:
Wanted: Fire-Heroes

A May 1887 issue of the *Albion New Era* mentions, "The burning of the Court House, and two extensive fires since, materially crippled our town … in spite of all it has been rebuilt after every fire."

You have to figure we're getting tired of that.

One reason Albionites finally organized might have been the progress other towns made in their own fire protection. In 1873, twelve miles away, Kendallville officials purchased a steam powered fire engine; in 1875, they hoisted a 600 pound fire bell over their fire hall; and in October, 1883, they paid $900 for a chemical fire engine. In 1877, after a series of fires, Columbia City firefighters received a steam engine.

As if to rub it in, in February, 1885, this ad appeared in area newspapers, including the *Albion New Era*: "If you want low rates of insurance, have a good Fire Department. This you can have by purchasing your fire apparatus of Rumsey and Co, Seneca Falls, NY."

Oh, sure. Now you tell us. (To this day, some people only support improved fire protection when told it might lower their insurance costs.)

The nearby town of Churubusco, apparently wanting low rates of insurance, bought a fire hose cart from that company in 1886, before their fire department was officially established the next spring. Several months after that the AFD would buy its hook and ladder wagon from the same company, as will be seen (spoiler alert!) later. Talk about a payback on your advertising investment.

Maybe jealousy of other towns provided an extra incentive, but the people of Albion did grow tired of seeing another row of buildings reduced to ashes on a seemingly regular schedule. Protecting a third new courthouse under construction, after the first one burned to the ground, may also have been a factor.

It became painfully obvious that water and buckets couldn't handle the job alone. In January 1885, bucket brigades managed to save Ray's Meat Market, owned not by Ray but by C.A. Howard, on South Orange Street. Albion citizens fought the fire in -12° temperatures, which added its own bucket full of problems. Considering the weather, it was a miracle the brigade could function at all, but they didn't make much of a save: The interior of the business was gutted, and its contents lost.

A month later, townspeople gathered again to discuss the state of the town's fire protection. The *Albion New Era* reported this shocker: "Nothing was done toward providing means to fight fires effectually, at the meeting Thursday night." (See, they had Thursdays back then.)

Even US politicians would slap their foreheads at this lack of progress.

By then no one seriously argued against a fire department, but about what type of apparatus to buy, how to organize the firefighting force, and – of course – how to pay for it all.

Organizers of the fledgling fire department found unlikely allies: arsonists. On February 12, 1885, came these short newspaper items: "The cry of fire emptied the skating rink on short notice Saturday night" … "The fire on Saturday night was undoubtedly the work of an incendiary." (**Incendiary** was the more printable term used for arsonists at the time.) It's possible someone was inventing that roller-skating-wheels-of-fire trick, but I doubt it.

Accidental fires were bad enough. With arson added into the mix, even the most skeptical townspeople were convinced of the need for an organized fire brigade. Or, maybe, the most skeptical got shouted down.

Progress at Last

In March 1887, a city in neighboring DeKalb County purchased a steam engine for $3,700, but a comment in the *Albion New Era* a month later showed that it takes more to run a fire department than just apparatus: "Auburn's new fire engine is about to be shipped to them, and they are at a loss to know where to keep it." Oops.

By then Albion had a designated fire chief, A.J. Denlar, and the problem wasn't lost on him or others planning Albion's fire department. They prepared a firehouse on West Main Street, along the south side of the courthouse square. It was probably little more than a small, wood frame garage, but when the fire engine arrived in early 1887, a place waited for it.

The next big problem: how to alert the firemen (sorry, no ladies back then, although there were some in other parts of the country) when a blaze broke out. The town of Albion had no radios, no sirens, no telephones. Waiting for the smell of smoke and the crackle of flames seemed counterproductive.

Townspeople had it covered: They held a "strawberry and ice cream festival" in the courtyard, July 1887. The proceeds purchased a fire alarm bell, which arrived in August and may be the same crud-incrusted bell now stored in the Albion Municipal Building. The *Albion New Era* explained that the bell was necessary so "Those who 'run with the machine' hear the summons to action in unmistakable tones." A week later: "The fire alarm bell was placed in position and tried. It works well, and produces a sound distinct from any other bell in town."

Well, it was shinier then ... At the time of this photo, what was probably Albion's first fire bell hung in the deteriorating tower of the 1930 Town Hall. Now it's at the town's municipal building, waiting to be cleaned up.

Until then, church bells across the community alerted townspeople to fires, which could get pretty confusing on a Sunday. The rest of the week, people would rush into the streets and look for smoke, or follow whoever appeared to know where they were going. By the time they found the blaze, it would be beyond their ability to control.

The fire alarm bell still didn't give the location of the fire, but it could be heard all over town and wouldn't be confused with other bells. It hung outside so anyone could ring it, but then the ringer had to wait at the firehouse, to tell the arriving volunteers where to go.

With an alarm system and firehouse in place, Albion welcomed its first **apparatus** – a word used to describe various kinds of firefighting vehicles to this day. Despite the urging of newspaper editors, the apparatus was not a hook and ladder, but a fire engine.

It wasn't powered by steam, or by chemicals, but by muscle. Steam engines took long minutes to get into operation, and the heavy equipment required three horses to pull them – and Albion's budget didn't allow for dedicated fire horses. Chemicals reacted to immediately "charge" a hose with pressurized water, but when the tank of chemicals ran out the apparatus became useless. But like all small communities, Albion had a plentiful supply of merchants, farmers, and other men with strong backs. That included, one would think, pesky newspaper editors who'd agitated for a fire department.

The fire engine is sometimes called a "pumper" in Indiana these days, although newer federal guidelines prefer the original term. It's the basic piece of firefighting apparatus that drafts water from a source, such as a cistern or pond, into a pump mounted on the truck, and then through another hose to the fire.

When first developed, hand pumps had to be supplied by bucket brigades, which dumped water into open-topped tubs in the apparatus. The nozzle was often mounted on the pump, which meant the bucket brigade still had to get dangerously close to the fire – as did the men who operated the pump. The advantage was that the stream of water could be aimed better and reached further than a tossed bucketful.

A simple length of leather, stitched shut to form a tube and tipped with brass couplings, changed all that. By the time Albion's engine arrived, fire hose was generally made of rubber, with a cotton jacket for strength, but the principle remained the same. The pump and its crew could stay back and pump water through hose to a brass nozzle, manned by a nozzleman and several hosemen who hauled it as close as heat and smoke would permit.

On the other end, a harder rubber hose would be dropped into a cistern, well or pond, to draft water into the engine just as one would suck soda through a straw. This eliminated the need for hundreds of people to form bucket brigades, although many of those people then went to work on the hand pump.

Albion's engine, which arrived a full year before the fire department gained official recognition, consisted of a wagon with two rows of handles called "brakes". Firefighters worked the brakes up and down to power a piston pump–say that three times fast–and the faster the volunteers worked the pump, the more water pressure it provided. The back breaking work had to continue for as long as water was needed.

On larger hand pumpers, dozens of men worked the brakes hundreds of times per minute, having to be replaced often as they became tired. Albion's pumper was much smaller, needing 8 to 10 men to operate at a time, although replacements would still need to stand by. It was a thankless and dangerous job, and the rapidly moving brakes broke many a firefighter's hand as he tried to take his place at the pump.

Modern fire engines are usually **Quads** – they carry a pump, hose, ground ladders, and a water tank. Albion's first pump was a single – just a pump – because otherwise it would be too heavy to draw by hand to the fire scene. As a result, the AFD's next major purchase needed to be a hose cart. It was pretty simple: a reel mounted on a two-wheeled cart. (Some cities used four-wheel hose wagons.) The standard fire hose at the time had a 2 ½ inch internal diameter; fifty foot sections of it, connected together with heavy brass couplings, would be wound around the reel.

It was a simple but revolutionary concept, like diet pop or the designated hitter: The engine company crew carried the hard suction hose and dropped it into their water supply; the hose company crew would run from the pump to the fire, reeling off their hose behind them as they went.

The town of Albion now had its apparatus, alarm system, fire hose, and plenty of eager volunteers. They didn't have an official fire department yet, as bureaucratic wheels grind slowly, but they stood ready to be tested.

Those tests would come soon enough.

Albion's second hose cart, or possibly even the first one … stay tuned as research continues.

"Rapid and Efficient Work"

Albion New Era, October 1, 1887. Headline: A LIVELY BLAZE!

"Last Monday at 12 o'clock, noon, just as people sat down to dinner, the violent and continued ringing of the fire alarm bell produced an instantaneous stampede and rush to the street.

"Only a few strokes of the bell were heard before the engine was seen flying south on Orange Street and it was ascertained that the house of John H. Frazure was on fire in its upper rooms. A violent wind was roaring from the Northwest, and the house being in an elevated position, received the full force of the gale, by which the flames were fanned so rapidly the upper part of the house was quickly burned out inside, so quickly that very little could be rescued."

(As an aside, I live on South Orange Street and the upper parts of my house show damage from a past fire. Coincidence? Probably.)

The account goes on to say all the home's contents – "fine clothing, beds, bedding, etc." – were destroyed. It also says:

"The Albion fire department boys did rapid and efficient work. A hill had to be climbed before reaching a position for efficient work, and the engine was hauled 'by hand' – yet they were on the ground playing upon the house before it was fairly understood there was a fire. There is no town of its size in the world that can beat Albion at a fire."

At first glance such high praise seems surprising. After all, fire gutted the upstairs and destroyed all the contents. But what would have happened a few months before, when no fire department yet existed? The upstairs wouldn't be gutted – the whole house would have burned to the ground, with nothing to stop a fire, in the wind described, from taking the whole neighborhood with it.

Also, the editor points out the challenge of firefighters pulling their engine – by hand – up a hill – for several blocks. Then they had to lay their hose, made of the much heavier stitched leather and brass instead of today's cotton, rubber, and lightweight couplings, from the nearest water supply. If they hoped to save the structure firefighters had to get close, battling heat and smoke with little or no protective clothing and no breathing protection. It took uncommon courage as well as a strong back, and still does today.

Add all this to the fact that the Albion firefighter of 1887 had no training or experience with his new equipment, and it's easy to see why the editor sang their praises.

A quick note on the owner of the burned home, John H. Frazure: In 1881, Frazure lost his restaurant to another fire. He co-owned that restaurant with a man named A.J. Denlar–who in 1887 became Albion's first fire chief. It's likely those two men were chief–pardon the pun–among those who pushed for an organized firefighting force.

Good Practice

Albion New Era, November 12, 1887: "On Wednesday last about ten o'clock the citizens of Albion were again startled by a fire alarm. The first sight that greeted people near the public square as they emerged from their houses was the fire engine dashing up Main Street toward the west part of town. Looking in that direction a dense volume of smoke was seen over the residence of Solomon

Hardenbrook, opposite the U.B. Church." (This would have been within a block or two of Chief Denlar's home.)

"The engine had to be taken into the back yard of the jail to get to the nearest cistern, about 300 feet north-east of the Hardenbrook house, with the jail building between; yet only about five minutes elapsed before they were ready to play water on the fire."

As it turned out, a single bucket of water knocked down the flames. At a signal from Chief Denlar, the hosemen turned the nozzle away and sent the stream down Main Street to avoid water damage inside the house. Back then they couldn't shut off the water at the nozzle (and in this case the pump worked 300 feet away, behind what is now the Old Jail Museum) so it took a moment to send word to the engine crew to stop "working the brakes".

This incident demonstrates a tradition important to the fire service ever since: Be prepared for the worst. It did no harm to have the volunteers and equipment ready to fight a major fire–in fact, it made for good practice, considering their lack of experience.

Albion New Era, November 25, 1887: "An alarm of fire at 9 o'clock Monday evening filled the streets with anxious crowd; but in a few minutes the welcome announcement was heard that the fire was 'out', and no damage was done, except an unpleasant smoking of the interior of E.J. Schwab's restaurant and of Schwab and Winans' Jewelry store – the fire being in the bakery, over in the basement under the restaurant.

"The Albion fire department boys were promptly on hand, as usual, and had their hose trained on the place in about five minutes."

This was a minor incident, rating no mention except in comparison to another fire in late September, 1883. Both fires started in the bakery portion of a restaurant operated by E.J. Schwab. The first fire, as mentioned earlier, leveled three structures and damaged two others. In the second fire, four years later, one building suffered minor smoke damage.

The Albion Fire Department has proved itself.

Hook & Ladder

So far we had an engine and a hose cart, but not the piece of equipment the *Albion New Era* called for thirteen years earlier. That arrived in January, 1888:

"Albion's new hook and ladder truck has arrived and it's a daisy. It was made at Seneca Falls, N.Y. The fire company is now amply provided with implements necessary to successfully battle with the fire fiend."

Albion's hook and ladder was manufactured by Rumsey and Co, the same company that placed ads in local papers several years before and also sold to the fledgling Churubusco Fire Department not far away. Obviously, it pays to advertise.

Today's ladder trucks sport hydraulic aerial ladders, able to reach over a hundred feet into the air. At the low end, they cost half a million dollars. But Albion's unit was no more than a long wagon, loaded with a variety of ground ladders, buckets, and some hand tools. The tallest ladder reached no higher than 35 feet and may have been shorter, although manufacturers made longer ones.

The ladder company members still needed hooks to pull down burning walls and protect neighboring structures from fire spread. But, since the volunteers now had a fighting chance to save the building where the fire started, the hooks could also tear apart interior ceilings and walls to find hidden fire, just as they do today.

At the invitation of Town Board Trustee Konkle, the *Noble County Democrat's* editor visited "Fireman's Hall", as he called the Albion firehouse, to see the new Hook and Ladder. He declared:

"It is a thing of beauty as well as utility. New, sound and symmetrical – built of the best materials, brightly painted and nickel plated, and furnished with ladders, hooks, poles, axes, crowbars and rubber buckets, all of the best style and workmanship, and every other appliance belonging to a first class outfit of the kind. It is a credit to the town and a monument to the liberal public spirit of its council and citizens."

No, no -- not that fancy. The Kendallville Fire Department's aerial ladder truck was invited over to help when the Albion feed mill caught fire. Albion's own hook and ladder went into service a century before, and went back out long before this.

Jeez, does the guy want to fight fires with it or marry it? But his admiration is in keeping with the great tradition of fire trucks as not just work machines, but beloved members of the firefighting community.

The same *Democrat* article, titled "Albion's fire-fighting weapons the best in this section", listed the men who ran with the Hook and Ladder Company:

John Epp, Foreman (the equivalent of today's captain.)

Alex Frazur

R. Hardenbrook

W.M. Frazur

Chas Haney

Frank Kimmel

Ed Alvord

W.J. Kennedy

J.B. Franks

H.M. Williams

N.B. Rogers

T.J. Anspaugh

(Whether the two Frazurs are related to the John Frazure of the earlier South Orange Street fire isn't clear; they were a huge family in Albion then, at a time when spelling wasn't high on a lot of priority lists. Kind of like today.)

The AFD stood equipped, manned, tested and ready - yet the organization had still not been made official.

The Worden House, almost lost during the courthouse fire, as seen from the southeast. The Quick Pix convenience store (also known as the Corner Stop) stands there now. People got very excited over big lumber back then. Photo courtesy the Old Jail Museum of Noble County.

CHAPTER THREE

Organization and Regulation
Or
The Job's Not Over 'Till the Paperwork's Done

MAY 3, 1888, Albion Town Board: "An ordinance for the Organization and regulation of a fire department in the incorporated Town of Albion in Noble County Indiana and prescribing penalties for the violation thereof."

(Maybe commas were in short supply back then.)

This lengthy ordinance spelled out the complete organization of the Albion Fire Department, which included records to be kept, expenses, and duties. The organizers tacked on at the end a number of fire prevention ordinances.

Officers included a chief, two assistant chiefs, and a foreman and assistant foreman (today's captain and lieutenant) for each separate company. They made provisions to organize several companies of each type (engine, hose, and ladder companies), but Albion's size and budget at the time precluded more than one of each.

The maximum membership of the fire companies was set at twenty for each hand engine company, fifteen for each hook and ladder company, and twelve for each hose company, including officers. The Albion Fire Department originally had about fifty members, plus three chiefs and six other officers, or about twice the membership of the AFD at the end of the Twentieth Century.

But in 1888, firefighting required more manpower than today. The size of Albion's pump isn't certain, but even the smallest hand-engine of the era took over half a dozen men to pump the engine.

The dozen hose company members pulled their rig to the fire and laid hose out at the scene. Then they had to haul the heavy, water filled hose close to the fire, pushing forward against the nozzle's back pressure. They had to be relieved as they went down from the effects of heat and smoke. Records around the country at the time are filled with accounts of dozens of firefighters at just one fire, laid out on the streets from smoke inhalation.

The duties of the hook and ladder men included placing ladders to reach the fire, bringing down trapped occupants, and accessing endangered roofs; using hand tools to expose hidden fire; and ventilating smoke and heat from the structure, so the hose crews could get close enough to extinguish the blaze.

Today it takes one firefighter to operate a pump. Lighter, more flexible hose is used, while protective gear, especially breathing air packs, increases safety and work time for interior crews. Saws, ventilation fans and other power equipment make fireground tasks faster and easier. The job of firefighting is still difficult, but modern equipment reduced manpower needs.

Manning a 2 1/2 inch diameter fire hose has changed little in the last century. (Here Albion and Noble Township firefighters work together at an 80s fire in Lutherhaven, a rural camp between their departments.)

Section 3 of the ordinance presents "Requisites for Membership":

"Every person to become a member of the fire department must, at the time of his election or appointment, be eighteen years of age, a citizen of the United States, a resident of Albion, Indiana, and able to converse understandingly in the English language, and shall possess such practical fitness and intellectual and physical capacity as may be considered requisite."

Later the minimum age increased to twenty-one before being reduced again, in 1978, to eighteen. Also, new members can now live anywhere in Albion's 96 square mile response area. Of course, they don't have to get to the firehouse on foot, or take the time to saddle a horse, but they do have to have a driver's license.

Section 5 reported all active members of the AFD "Shall be exempt from working upon the streets of said town, and shall not be liable to pay commutation for such labor." This perk isn't so surprising, since at one point in history the Army exempted firefighters from being drafted. On the other hand, volunteer firefighters made up some military units during the Civil War (including the famous New York Zouaves).

Section 5 also stated that the fire chief would keep two books: One "a complete list … of all officers and men in service as full members of the FD."

The second book was a record of fires, which seems simple enough. But that list would include, for every fire call: "The date, time, location, class of building, name of owner, name of occupant, use, cause of fire, personal injuries or death of firemen or citizens, amount of loss on buildings, amount of loss on goods and fixtures, total loss, his estimate of the value of the property immediately before being injured or destroyed, and amount of insurance on property as near as he can ascertain."

Those of you who tend to read out loud can catch your breath now. Believe it or not, run reports are just as complicated today, if not more so.

The chief was also responsible for the town's public wells and cisterns, the main source of water. He had to see that "they are kept constantly supplied with water and in good working order, and prevent water from being taken there from, except at fires."

Of course, the chief's position was (and still is) a great responsibility. Town fathers deemed the job so important the chief had to "Give bond in the sum of one thousand dollars, said bond to be made payable to the Board of Trustees … and be conditioned for the faithful discharge of duty". The deputy chiefs, secretary, and treasurer also gave bond, to guarantee they wouldn't mishandle town resources.

The AFD expected its members to be at every fire, whether it meant leaving work, meals, or sleep. The acceptable excuse for absence was illness or being out of town, at a time when people didn't leave town often. Violation of that rule brought a one dollar fine to any man who wanted to remain on the department – big money, back then.

So, what did the firefighter expect to receive, in return for his service?

Not only did he not get paid, but he did the paying -- dues of five cents per month to the department.

Sharp lines divided the three companies: "No member shall be permitted to transfer his membership from one Company to another without first paying all dues, fines and charges in the company to which he was formerly a member." It took special permission to transfer membership, so if you became a member of the hook and ladder company, then discovered your fear of heights, you were pretty much left hanging … so to speak.

On the fireground, the chief could commandeer the aid of any citizen, "team and vehicle", and level a $5 fine for interfering with an officer or firefighter performing his duty. The same fine applied to defacing any piece of fire apparatus, plus damages. Running over hose brought a $5-$10 penalty, plus liability for damage done to hose and engine. Speaking as a person who once had a fire hose pulled right out of my hand by a speed demon driver, hanging's too good for 'em.

Running over a hose causes a backwash of pressure, called water hammer, which can damage a fire pump, burst hose, and injure firefighters. Plus, it's really impolite.

The hook and ladder company could lawfully "cut down and remove any building, erection, or fence for the purpose of checking (stopping) the progress of the fire." Besides that, the chief could use explosives to blow up a structure for the same purpose, so it was a good idea to be on good terms with him.

Memories stayed sharp of fires, both in small towns and big cities, that burned whole blocks, jumped streets, and in the case of the Great Chicago Fire, even jumped across rivers.

At a time when every building had at least one fireplace or wood stove, the safe disposal of ashes was vital. Embers could smolder in piles of ash for hours, then burst out to cause a conflagration (which you'll recall means Big Honkin' Fire). The ordinance ordered that no ashes could be kept or deposited in town unless in a "close or secure vessel, or brick or stone ash room". Violators could be fined $3, plus another dollar a day until they properly looked after their ashes.

To this day, fires are still caused by hot ashes dumped into trash cans or cardboard boxes, so you can see why the town fathers wanted people to calm their ashes down.

The final paragraph of the ordinance dealt with the day's hazardous materials. The term "HazMat" became a catch phrase in the 1980s, but the problem has always been around. It led to the law that no one could keep, in any one place, "more than five forty gallon barrels of crude petroleum, gasoline, naphtha, benzene, camplfene, spirit gas, burning fluid, or spirits of turpentine, or more than two 25 pound canisters of gunpowder." They were to be kept in tin or other metal canisters, and the fine for a violation was a whopping $1-$10.

These days, it takes a book to list all the exotic hazardous materials firefighters may be faced with at an emergency scene. So there is one: the Emergency Response Guidebook, which lists thousands of hazardous chemicals and good rules of thumb, such as "Don't get your thumb burned off". The materials listed in the ordinance seem tame by comparison, but back then they had no firefighting foam or dry chemical, and so no way to deal with flammable liquid: plain water would make the situation worse.

Of course, 200 gallons of flaming gasoline would still destroy whatever it was stored in, but with luck and fast work such a fire could be prevented from taking the rest of the neighborhood with it.

If today's construction, transportation and other interests had lobbies back then, there'd have been arguments and politicking over the fine points of town ordinance No. 44, but no one considered arguing over the ordinance as a whole. The Albion Fire Department was ready to spend the next century battling the "fire fiend".

But its fire chief wouldn't live to see it.

First Chief

Like Moses, Albert J. Denlar led his people to the Promised Land, but would not live to see them cross over.

Denlar, a native of Germany, was born in 1845, one hundred years before Germany surrendered to the Allies in World War 2. (Another source lists his actual place of birth as Switzerland, but on that question the Swiss didn't want to get involved.)

He arrived in America in 1851, and at some point not long after his father, a sailor, drowned. Denlar's mother remarried and the family moved to Fairfield County, Ohio, but for some reason Denlar hit the road at the age of 13. Unable to get along with his step-father? A lack of space in the new household? Wanderlust? Whatever happened, he ended up in Indiana, and trained as a baker in Columbia City.

Soon he hit the road again, and gained employment with the B&O Railroad just in time for their construction of a new line, which took him to Albion in 1873. After the construction he moved back to Columbia City, but returned to Albion a few years after that.

On his second move to Albion he opened that restaurant with John Frazure – the restaurant that burned down in one of those big, block sweeping fires. The Frazures were a big family in Albion, and originally owned the entire neighborhood around my own South Orange Street home. It was mostly empty lots at the time, and they either built my house in the late 1870s, or owned the property when it was built.

It's not certain if the fire that destroyed the restaurant of Denlar & Frazure is what made Denlar want to fight fires, but it's not unusual for a small town department to get new volunteers that way. In any case he had more than business on his mind, because in 1874 he married – her last name will seem familiar – Miss Alice F. Frazure.

That settled him down: They had three children (Melvin, Catherine, and Leona) in their West Main Street home as Denlar served as a member of Albion's

Town Board and joined the Masonic order. By the time Albion's firefighters organized, he had gained enough respect in town to be named fire chief.

But on April 10, 1888, twenty-three days before the Albion Town Board passed the ordinance that officially founded the Albion Volunteer Fire Department, Denlar passed away of unknown causes. (That is, unknown to me.) The volunteers draped the engine house in black, and buried him in section A, lot 6, of what is now Rose Hill Cemetery.

He was 42 years old.

Albion's first Fire Chief has a simple headstone in Albion's Rose Hill Cemetery, not far west of where his Main Street home was.

CHAPTER FOUR

The Early Years
Or
From Hand to Horse to Flying Machines

The next recorded Chief of the Albion Fire Department, according to 1894 insurance records, was Albion druggist and later Noble County Treasurer William E. Worden. That's his family whose hotel was saved during the Noble County Courthouse fire, so you can be sure he understood the value of an organized fire department.

But an organized fire department didn't mark the end of major fires, by any means. For one thing, the new equipment – although state of the art to the small town residents – wasn't really enough to handle a major fire.

To compare, Albion's 1952 engine would supply two 2 ½ inch diameter attack hoselines at full capacity, while the 2000 model can supply at least five. Since 1952, Albion has had – with short interruptions – three engines in service at all times. In 1888 they had one, and it could handle one relatively weak water stream from one hoseline.

Once a fire advanced, the volunteers still had to concentrate on nearby exposures, to protect property not yet burned. Even without an exposure nearby, the AFD didn't have the capability to knock down advanced fires in large buildings.

An example was the Askew & Miller Planing Mill, which burned to the ground near the turn of the century. The industry was over 30 years old, large, flammable, and used for a hazardous occupation.

The fire started at around 3:30 a.m., when no one was around, and made good headway before being discovered. All those factors ensured its destruction.

The AFD responded and did the only thing they could – protect exposures. No doubt the hose company crew ran themselves to exhaustion, trying to keep one hoseline in operation to protect everything around the property.

Inside the building two boats were destroyed, one belonging to the "Blue Gill Club". One can only guess at the club's vocation. The other boat remained under construction, and became a source of controversy: Samual Foster had been employed to build two boats, one for a man named Heitt, and the other for Frank Prickett. With no insurance on the contents, each man insisted the burned boat belonged to the other.

No one arrived at a solution. More ominously, no one ever discovered how the fire started. The local fish all had alibis.

Water Supply, and Other Improvements

At the turn of the century, the town of Albion experienced rapid change. The population rose to 1,350, and as the town grew, so did its fire protection needs.

Workers replaced cisterns with water mains in 1895, and a 1901 fire insurance map of Albion shows two miles of 4 to 10 inch diameter mains that fed 24 hydrants, scattered across town. Water pressure topped off at 100 pounds per square inch (psi) – better than the pressure today! But that's misleading, because the mains were smaller, and not as well interconnected (**gridded**, which means water flowed in from more than one direction). Once a hydrant was opened and water started flowing, the pressure dropped quickly.

There was also the question of how much volume would be available. I can find no mention of a water tower before one went up during the Great Depression (it was dismantled just a few years ago). It's possible the water came directly from wells, pressurized by a pump but limited in its capacity.

Still, the volunteers now had two dozen new sources of pressurized water, in addition to cisterns that remained in place, some into the late 60s. In fact, at least two of the original courthouse cisterns remained there, buried under the streets, until workers removed them as part of a courthouse square improvement project in 2009.

Since some areas of Albion still stood too far from the nearest hydrant, the town fathers purchased another hose cart. Together the two carts carried 800 feet of 2 ½ inch hose, enough to reach most properties.

That one acquisition forced the AFD out of its quarters, after just ten years. Just before the turn of the 19th Century the town constructed a narrow but long wooden firehouse on South Orange Street, between Main and Hazel, just south of the later location of the Albion Town Hall. The AFD would occupy that block, on the east side of the street, for over sixty years.

Since there are no known pictures of Albion's first two firehouses, here's the most recent one, under construction in 1997. What? My time machine was in the shop.

In addition to the alarm bell, which remained in use for some time, an alarm whistle was hoisted up on the town's water works. Any volunteer in town who didn't hear one would certainly hear the other.

Another Conflagration

Both alarms went to work on May 2, 1901, when Mother Nature rudely reminded Albionites that even the best fire department could do nothing about wind.

A gusty breeze blew to the southwest at 2 p.m. when the firefighters turned out for a blaze in the barn of B.F. Easly, a drayman, located near the northwest corner of the courthouse square. A **drayman** is a hauler of various goods, probably to and from the railroad, so it can be assumed his wagon was inside.

Windblown flames soon spread across an alley south to the barn of Ransom Harkins, then southeast to another barn owned by M.H. Kimmel, and east to Elijah Lloyd's cooper shop. To the northwest, fire partially gutted the Presbyterian parsonage, and damaged several other homes downwind.

B.F. Easly was one of the first on the scene. He rescued his brother-in-law's horse from the barn, then returned for his own horse, and managed to lead it to the door before it panicked and refused to go further. Easly, eyebrows and moustache burned off and hands blistered, escaped, while the horse collapsed from smoke inhalation and died in the fire.

The firefighters could deploy at most three hoselines, two of which furnished weak streams from hydrant pressure alone. It's hard to imagine the stress they must have been under - especially the officers, who had to decide which areas to protect and which to sacrifice.

Albion's *Noble County Democrat* sang the praises of the town's six year old water main and hydrant system: "Once more has the water works paid for itself many times. If Albion had not had water works, one third of the town would now be a desolate waste."

Too true, and the paper acknowledged that the presence of water alone didn't stop the fire. "Simon Schloss desires The *Noble County Democrat* to extend thanks to those who assisted in saving his property … great praise and credit should be given to the fire department and all others, who so nobly and heroically assisted in putting out the fire and saving household goods. Many of them braved danger and even death in their efforts to give assistance."

Hot off the Presses

A fire on the first of March, 1903, almost extinguished one of the *Noble County Democrat's* competitors: "A small blaze in the *Albion New Era* office this forenoon made things lively in that quarter for a short time. The fire caught in some paper back of the stove in the press room. It was extinguished before much damage was done however." If the fire got much bigger, the AFD would have had its chance to defend freedom of the press.

Is Rome Burning?

Of course, the larger fires attract the most interest, and a 1905 fire in Rome City had Albion in an uproar. On a Saturday evening in March, a rumor circulated that the entire town of Rome City, ten miles away, was burning. But as people organized to lend assistance, word came that the fire was not in Rome City itself, but in the nearby Barber woods.

The fire destroyed two cottages and damaged several others, but Rome City citizens managed to control the blaze before it spread into the town itself. Getting Albion's hand drawn fire equipment to the scene, loaded onto heavy, slow wagons, would be a feat in itself.

True or False

In some cities false alarms are an everyday problem. In Albion they're uncommon, but the town's first was recorded in April of 1907. At 7 p.m. the fire alarm went off and the volunteers hurried to the station, but they found no sign of flames or people. They determined the alarm's electric wires must have been crossed by the wind, setting off the whistle. Thank goodness it didn't cause a fire.

Thoughtless Persons

A problem both more common and more serious than false alarms is ground cover fires. In Indiana they're usually called grass fires, but the category covers grass, brush, swamp, field and woodlands. Then, as today, they're often caused by sparks from trash and brush pile fires, or people burning off fence rows. When such fires began outside town limits their discovery was often delayed; and with no telephones or radios, so was turning in an alarm –assuming the blaze happened close enough to town for the volunteers to even get their apparatus there.

At the time, before rural homes became more common, the fires often burned themselves out without damaging more than corn or wheat fields. Sometimes they reached structures, with predictable results. After one particularly bad summer, the *Wolf Lake Trolly* printed this on October 22, 1908:

"Thoughtless persons who set fire at any time of the year might profit by a reading of the statue following: Whoever maliciously or wantonly sets fire to any woods or to anything growing or being upon marsh, prairie or grounds, not his own property, or maliciously or wantonly permits any fire to pass from his own marsh, prairie or grounds, to the injury or destruction of the property of any other person, shall on conviction be fined not less than five dollars, nor more than one hundred dollars, to which may be added imprisonment in the county jail not exceeding thirty days."

Do you ever wonder how local statutes might read if those who wrote them read them out loud? Without taking a breath?

It's doubtful many people heeded the warning, since grass and field fires remain a major problem across the country to this day.

Although small fires, extinguished by property owners or firefighters before the blazes got out of control, continued to plague Albion, the town spent the next several years without a major conflagration. If the quiet lulled the good citizens into a false sense of security, they had only to look at the newspapers of May 5, 1908, to remind them of what could happen.

Fort Wayne's New Aveline Hotel, at the corner of Calhoun and Berry streets, caught fire at 3:30 a.m. Fire gutted the six story hotel and left only the outside walls standing the next day. Twenty-five people lost their lives.

Although no structures of that size stood in Albion, the town's firefighters knew the danger, and that the death of a firefighter or civilian could occur at any moment. After hearing of the Fort Wayne fire, they checked over their equipment, trained harder, crossed their fingers, and listened for the fire whistle.

The Paragon Mills Fire

The further a fire department gets from the last Big One, the closer it is to the next.

Owned in 1911 by A.L. Shipley, John W. Earle, and Frederick Barnes, the Paragon Mills did a booming business. Not only did the people of Albion go there, but according to the *Albion New Era*: "Out of town trade has been limited only by the capacity of the mills. Paragon flour has become a household word in the entire district it covered."

Three mills stood on the site at South and Third streets: a flouring mill, a saw mill, and a planing mill. (A planing mill turns boards from a sawmill into finished dimensional lumber.)

The fire hazard for such an operation is severe to begin with (flour dust is explosive, for instance), but two other details added to the fire's seriousness: The blaze began at 2 a.m., which delayed its discovery, and it appeared to be the work of an arsonist.

Although so busy it ran some nights, the mill was closed at the time the fire broke out. "Those working at the mill insist there was no hot box," The *Albion New Era* reported. "The origin of the fire was in the southwest portion of the mill away from the locality where spontaneous combustion would likely occur."

Around 9:30 p.m., three hours after the mill closed, Shipley entered the building to retrieve papers left by Earle, and at the time all appeared normal: "There was no smell of burning oil as would be occasioned by a hot box; there was no pungent smoke odor; no stifling air to induce spontaneous combustion."

As Shipley sat at his home across the street from the mill an hour later, he heard someone outside, apparently looking into the house. But, thinking it had been his son, he retired for the night soon after – only to discover his son already asleep in bed. Around 11 p.m. a buggy passed Earle's home, and drove twice around the block. (A buggy out at that hour would be pretty unusual for 1911.) At about the same time, another town resident noticed no light shone at the mill, and an hour later another man also noticed it dark.

Later the workers at the plant all agreed the mill closed up as usual, two hours before the fire was discovered. But when Shipley ran across the street to save the business' books and papers, he saw a large door on the north end partially open.

Firefighters turned out in force, but soon realized nothing could be done about the burning flour mill. They turned their water streams on the planing and saw mills and managed to save them, although severe radiant heat damaged the structures. The blaze destroyed 80 barrels of flour, almost 2,000 bushels of grain, and 1,100 bushels of wheat.

Sometimes overhauling and investigating a fire can be like finding a needle in a ... oh, never mind.

Another 200 barrels of flour had shipped out the day before, but total damage still amounted to $120,000.

Some townsfolk were doubtful, but the owners remained so convinced of the fire's cause they offered a $500 reward to be "given to anyone who can produce evidence that will lead to the conviction of the person or persons who caused or instigated the fire at the Paragon Mills, Albion, Ind., on Wednesday, August 16, 1911."

But no one was ever convicted of the crime, and no reason found why someone would want to burn the mill. Maybe the culprits wanted to go gluten free?

Bells, whistles, and word of mouth alerted Albion volunteers to fires, but in late 1913 an unusual alarm system saved a home.

The history of powered air flight was just ten years old at this point. World War I, the conflict that turbocharged aircraft development, remained a year off. An airplane overhead would be rare, to say the least.

Yet as an airplane was literally "just passing" over Albion late that year the pilot noticed a small fire, caused by an overheated chimney, on the roof of the W.H. Favinger home. When one of those newfangled airborne contraptions made low circles over the house it attracted a great deal of attention, including that of the home's occupants.

The AFD turned out, and doused the flames within moments. Since no landing strip waited nearby the pilot flew on, and the home's occupants never got to thank their flying fire alarm. Who knows? With the Wright Brothers company one state over, maybe one of their pilots manned this particular aircraft.

No airplane sounded the alarm when fire broke out two days later on the roof of the Mort Bennet farm, on the south edge of town. This blaze wasn't noticed until a passerby alerted the occupants. By the time the hand drawn fire apparatus arrived flames engulfed the roof, and only a great deal of hard, fast work saved the rest of the house.

It's a good example of what a difference can be made when a fire is discovered and reported quickly.

Growth

By 1914 the population of Albion had grown to 1,600. Workers installed another mile and a half of water mains, which added only two more hydrants but increased pressure from 100 to 120 psi. That's more than the normal operating pressure of today, but if firefighters wanted to deploy more than one hoseline, they still had to couple it directly to a hydrant.

How to reach fires in outlying areas of town remained a problem, so the volunteers obtained a third hose cart, which gave the AFD a total of 1,800 feet of hose.

(A note of amateur historian caution, here. Information is sparse from back then, and a 1914 insurance map that shows three hose carts might be wrong. Two of Albion's hose carts still exist, so if the mapmakers meant to show two carts and the hand engine -- then one of those existing carts is the original one from the AFD's founding.)

The number of firefighters dropped to 36 men, but when the bell and whistle sounded most of the townspeople still turned out to give what assistance they could, including help to operate the hand pump.

Knowing the importance of early alerts, town fathers experimented for a time with twelve fire alarm boxes, positioned around town. Operated over telegraph wires, the boxes sent a signal to the fire station when someone pulled the handles. Each box tapped out a different number which advised the volunteers of the approximate location of the fire. They remained in service until the early 1920s when the telephone came into general use.

Albion's fire protection continued to improve, and even though the apparatus were still hand drawn and operated, the townspeople stood proud. Albionites seemed safer than ever from the "fire fiend", as many still called uncontrolled fires.

My Kingdom for a Horse

Then, sometime in 1914, disaster struck. Exactly what happened – mechanical breakdown, accident – isn't recorded, but the hand operated pump, Albion's only fire engine, became unusable.

(Take into consideration what I said earlier, which is that I could just be wrong. I'd prefer to think not. But remember, the engine was twenty-six years old, so sudden failure was a distinct possibility – and we do know that a call went out at that time for a new engine.)

The loss must have been sudden, because no arrangements had been made to replace it. Technology continued to advance. What kind of engine best suited Albion? Another hand operated pump, chemical, steam, or one of those newfangled gasoline powered vehicles? What size should it be? What company should it be purchased from?

Volunteers continued to fight fires, coupling their hoses directly to the hydrant for the 120 psi hydrant pressure. Because of friction loss, the "stretch" of hose couldn't be too long before the stream reduced to a trickle, but it was better than nothing. The hook & ladder company pulled down fences, roofs and walls to stop flame spread, so firefighters lost individual buildings, but prevented conflagrations.

Meanwhile, Albionites agreed on the type of apparatus they wanted. They still had to unravel red tape, just as we do now. Bids had to be advertised and accepted, public meetings held, and paperwork sent to the state capitol. To everyone's great relief, the new apparatus arrived in early 1917, after three whole years without one.

Evidently the town fathers thought delivering water straight from the hydrant to the fires worked pretty well, because the new unit wasn't a pumper at all. Costing $1,700, the horse drawn wagon carried two 35 gallon chemical tanks, a 100 foot reel of 1 inch rubber hose that delivered chemically propelled water to the fire, and a bed full of 2 ½ inch hose to bring water from the hydrant to the wagon.

A **chemical engine** has no pump: Water pressure is created by the reaction of chemicals together, much as carbonated soda will shoot out of a bottle when it's shaken. In fact, Kendallville citizens named their chemical engine "the soda fountain".

Chemical engines had a limited advantage. They didn't need dozens of men operating the pump to pressurize water, as with the hand engine. While a steam engine delivered a great deal more water without the need for large amounts of manpower, it took several minutes to heat the water boiler and build up pressure. A chemical engine could deliver water rapidly, and maybe quench the blaze before it grew out of control. It's an early example of what firefighters today call a quick-attack apparatus.

But the chemicals fed through one small diameter fire hose, which didn't deliver enough water to absorb the heat of a large blaze, and once the chemicals ran out the engine became useless. In larger communities, fire companies often ran with both a chemical engine and a steam engine, to use the advantages of both. Without the money for that the volunteers had to choose, and decided the risk was worth the chemical engine's advantages.

Dough, Boys

Then, as now, most of the AFD's budget came from tax money, and the emergency purchase of a $1,700 engine caused a financial strain. Besides taxes, funds came from two other areas: Townships outside Albion city limits paid for every response into their areas, and the firemen still paid dues.

But in 1916 Albion received just $6 for runs outside town. Until 1917 the volunteers still responded on foot, so response time made calls outside town limits a hopeless exercise. Even if the fire was within running distance, they could do little unless there was a pond or lake nearby from which to draft water.

Meanwhile, firemen's dues amounted to $101 in 1919, an amount offset by the decision to compensate firefighters for their time.

Over the years the number of volunteers dropped, partially because of local boys who went off to World War I, and a flu epidemic that killed hundreds of millions at the end of the war. The other reasons were economical. While they trained, held meetings, maintained equipment, and responded to calls, the volunteers lost personal time and sleep. Most employers let their people go to fires, knowing they might need help themselves someday, but the volunteers lost pay when they left. As the number of calls increased, some volunteers couldn't afford to leave work – but if they didn't, the department fined them for not showing up.

In order to make up the difference, the Town Board decided to pay each volunteer 50 cents for the first hour they spent on a call, and 25 cents for each subsequent hour. Dues seemed a little silly after that, so the practice was soon dropped.

The new engine brought further costs. Water was free; the chemicals cost money. The AFD itself didn't own horses, and had to pay each time they hitched up the nearest two animals to make a response. Not all horses are trained or capable of pulling wagons, and from time to time they'd have to deal with an ill-tempered animal. Also, because with horses the firefighters could respond further out of town, the number of calls outside town limits shot upward.

In 1919, a tax of 8 cents for every $100 assessed valuation paid for new fire hydrants and mains. But town fathers knew if they didn't take action soon, they might face another emergency when it came time to replace the chemical engine. They decided the best way to pay for new apparatus would be to charge for the present one, and an ordinance was posted by the Albion Town Board on November 12, 1919:

"Ordinance Fixing Rate of Pay for Use of Chemical Engine, Etc., Outside Corporate Limits.

"… For the use of the chemical engine, One Dollar and Fifty Cents charged for each mile necessarily traveled, the invoice price of all chemicals used plus freight and dray; that the members of the Albion Fire Department be paid at the rate of Fifty Cents per hour for the first hour and Twenty Five Cents per hour for each addition hour, for each member attending fire."

For Albion firefighters horse drawn firefighting wouldn't last long, and they skipped the steam engine era entirely.

Albion firefighters set up a helicopter landing zone and help load a patient they've freed from an auto accident – technology the founders of the AFD couldn't have imagined.

CHAPTER FIVE

The 1920s:
Changes and mechanization
Or,
Those Newfangled Thingamajigs

The chemical engine became Albion's first "fully equipped" apparatus, designed to fight a fire without relying on auxiliary equipment. In other words, it carried not only the means to pressurize water, but also hose, ladders, hooks, and hand tools. Why not? Instead of being drawn by the firefighters themselves, it was a two horsepower vehicle. Nobody asked the horses.

So, with AFD manpower down to about 33 men by the 20s, the hook & ladder wagon was retired. It marked the end of the "company" system, which divided the AFD into hose, engine, and hook & ladder companies, each with a separate organization and separate members.

By the end of the decade, each firefighter trained to handle any fireground job: whoever got there at the right time could lay hose or operate a nozzle, raise ladders, perform rescues, and ventilate. What a firefighter did at the scene depended on when he got there, and what needed to be done first.

Three hundred feet of hose fit on the chemical engine's hose bed. With 1,100 feet more on the hose reels, the AFD had 1,400 feet available. All of this was 2 ½ inch diameter hose, plus 100 feet of 1 inch hose carried on a reel above the chemical tanks.

To compare, minimum standards a century later called for 1,200 feet on each fire engine. AFD engines carry more, with diameters of 5, 3, and 1 3/4, to handle a variety of jobs. Two and a half inch, the standard size at the turn of the last century, wasn't enough to carry a good amount of water long distances from the hydrant due to friction loss. Don't get me started on the "stretch" around corners and up stairs to reach some small, smoldering mattress fire.

Two of the hose carts now carried 500 feet each. The third – now almost thirty years old – had only 100 feet, and rarely saw use. The last of Albion's three original fire apparatus, it vanished into history, although the newest hose cart has been reconditioned and is in an Albion town storage building. The third is stored at the Old Jail Museum, about a block from the location of the original fire station.

The changes were far from over. In 1925 John Gatwood became chief of the AFD, and presided over one of the most exciting periods of growth since the department's formation.

Engine Problems

By the mid-twenties, the firefighters became more and more disenchanted with the chemical engine; although it was perfect for fast attacks on small fires, more advanced blazes spelled trouble. The engine wouldn't flow enough water for enough time to contain the kind of conflagrations that struck all communities. They needed an apparatus able to pump a continuous stream.

Gasoline powered fire engines had been built as early as the turn of the century, and proved so reliable that over time they replaced every other kind of apparatus. Gasoline pumps could flow more water, at higher pressure, for more time, than any rig in Albion's experience.

They were also less expensive than horses, and easier to clean up after.

In fact, as more people bought automobiles, horses became hard to come by in an emergency. Unlike horses, a gasoline powered engine didn't poop out, so to speak, before it reached distant fires. It didn't take time to get the pressure up (in the engine boiler, not the horse), as with steam engines.

That, and no gasoline rig ever got spooked by fire, as happened with untrained "volunteer" fire horses.

While new truck talk intensified, several fires in early 1929 demonstrated the problems of fire protection in those days. One, at the A.E. Jones farm a mile and a half north of Albion, wiped out an entire farm.

The blaze started when Mrs. Jones fell in the barn with a lit lantern – pretty much the same way the Great Chicago Fire started, depending on whose story you believe. Barns burned then as fast as they do today, and this one became engulfed within minutes.

As described in the *Albion New Era*, a strong wind from the south carried "flying cinders to the machine shed and house. Fast work got all the livestock from the barn and part of the furniture from the house. All the farm buildings were consumed except two small buildings which were out of the line of flying cinders."

Also lost: "most of the machinery and farm implements, and a threshing separator belonging to Ollie Former." (I threw that comma in there; the century old style of writing leaves me breathless.)

On being called, the AFD ran into a problem that would plague them for decades – lack of water. The frustrated firefighters had only enough to keep the two small outbuildings from catching fire from radiant heat.

A similar problem faced fire units from Albion, Wolcottville, and Cromwell when part of Wawaka's downtown burned. Wawaka, in northwest Noble County, is several miles from any of those communities, and has no fire department of its own.

Albion sent the chemical engine, and the three departments managed to save K.L. Kitchen's store, which received slight damage. But two buildings belonging to the Weaver estate – a barber shop and a restaurant – burned. No doubt the disaster reminded volunteers of past incidents in their own towns.

A Case of Gas

This convinced the Albion Town Board, and in July, 1929, board members Walter F. Carver, John F. Gatwood, and Fred B. Moore advertised for bids on a

The '29 leaves the 1930 firehouse on its way to a steamroller fire on the courthouse square. Yes, a steamroller fire. (Still photo from a video courtesy Bill Shultz and the Noble County Historical Society.)

new fire truck. The fact that Gatwood was both a Town Board member and the fire chief didn't hurt the efforts.

They advertised for a "Triple Combination Fire Apparatus, pumping engine, chemical engine and hose motor car, capacity not less than 300 gallons per minute, all to be mounted on 1 ½ ton chassis, to be lettered and labeled as directed by the board."

What? Another chemical engine? Some still didn't trust that newfangled gasoline power. Although it boasted a 300 gpm gas pump, the truck also came with a 35 gallon chemical tank that could pressurize the 250 gallons of on-board water without the use of the gas engine.

The truck was made by the Buffalo Fire Appliance Co., of New York, which mounted it on a Chevy chassis. The old hand pump, hose cart and hook & ladder were "singles"; although advertised as a triple combination unit, the '29 was actually a **Quad** by modern standards, as it carried hose, pump, water tank and ladders. Like the chemical engine, in theory it needed no other apparatus to back it up.

The truck carried 100 feet of 1 inch rubber "booster" hose connected to the chemical tank, 450 feet of 2 ½ inch hose, ladders, a "pike" pole with a hook at the end, other hand tools and, of course, the pump and water tank. Between the two of them, the gas powered pumper and the chemical engine carried 48 feet of ladders. Not all in one ladder, of course. Let's not get silly.

In the style of the day, the truck's cab had no roof or doors – which made for some cold winter responses. Two firefighters could sit, but the normal engine company complement at the time ranged from 5-8 men: The other 3-5 people stood on the running and tail boards, and held onto cross bars. Nobody ever said firefighting was a safe business.

The closest this writer ever got to getting killed on a fire call was while riding the "back step" on the way to a fire, thanks to a combination of energetic driving and a bump in the road. We don't do that anymore.

"Frantic Appeals"

New trucks arrive under one of two circumstances: either they introduce a slow period for fire activity, or all hell breaks loose. The '29 was a few months old in February, 1930, when it responded to a blaze reminiscent of those that plagued Albion's early history.

Flames burned several buildings to the ground in the southwest Noble County community of Wolf Lake, and threatened the entire eastern half of the town. It would have been a cold trip, riding the back step of a fire truck for a dozen miles, but the firefighters had to have been glad they didn't need to wait on horses to pull them the entire way.

The *Albion New Era's* account of the fire contained a report not complimentary of other area fire departments:

"Frantic appeals were made to the fire departments of Albion, Ligonier, Cromwell and Churubusco, but only Albion responded. The others refused to come and naturally, the citizens of Wolf Lake are not pleased with the treatment they received from the fire departments that refused to leave their own boundaries."

Firefighters today would be horrified at the thought. Their idea is simple: If somebody calls, you come. Maybe those other departments still had horse drawn apparatus, and thought they couldn't get there quickly enough to do any good. Maybe elected officials refused to let their fire departments leave the area in fear of a fire of their own, or in an effort to save money. Let's face it, there are politicians to this day who would think about money or politics, even in the face of emergency appeals. Whatever the reason, only Albion firefighters showed up; it's not hard to get a crew of firefighters to go anywhere, if it allows them to put a brand new truck to work.

Such incidents spawned the **mutual aid** agreements in use today. Local fire departments pledge to send their neighbors help whenever called on, in return of a guarantee of such help in return. It all tends to even out.

Cold remains an enemy of firefighters. Here a deluge nozzle is draped in ice at the South Orange Street Bakery fire.

The *Albion New Era* added, "The Albion exchange was also highly complimented for promptness and assistance." At about that time, as telephones came into general use in the area, the town took Albion's 12 fire alarm boxes out of service. A similar revolution goes on today, as cell phones replace hard wired telephone systems.

On the same night as the Wolf Lake fire, another blaze broke out in Merriam, south of Albion and only a few miles from Wolf Lake. It wasn't reported if any fire departments responded to the Roy Rapp farm, where flames destroyed his residence and killed about 400 young chickens. Any local firefighters permitted to leave their towns were already occupied in Wolf Lake, so it's unlikely there was any help to be had.

When it rains it pours, especially with a new fire truck in service. (You'd think a pouring rain would help firefighters, wouldn't you? In reality, it usually just makes their job more miserable.) On the first Saturday of May that year, a cottage owned by a Fort Wayne man burned at Skinner Lake, east of Albion. With him away, the fire got a good head start before a neighbor discovered it.

By the time she turned in the alarm flames engulfed the small building, and when Albion's new pumper arrived its main job was to protect another cottage nearby, which ended up with $50 damage.

This time firefighters had plenty of water, from the nearby lake, but delayed discovery doomed the cottage.

Each new apparatus Albion received was larger than the one it replaced, as they became motorized, more powerful, and better equipped. After 30 years, the department grew out of its firehouse.

In fact, when the '29 first arrived it wasn't housed in the fire station at all.

Ernie Leatherman, who remembers the horse drawn chemical engine, recalls that the '29 was initially stored in Braden Sales, the Chevy dealership where his father, Dan, worked as a head mechanic. (In addition to being chief mechanic, Dan Leatherman was also a volunteer.)

The Chevy garage was on the south side of Main Street, in a building later occupied by the Noble REMC that currently serves as the Central Noble Schools Superintendent's Office. For all intents, it became a temporary fire station.

Imagine how exciting that must have been to young Ernie Leatherman, to be hanging around at the age of 9 where his father worked – along with the town's brand new fire engine, which his father drove for the department. That's childhood memories for you.

The town's government also grew, but had nowhere to grow to – in fact, for the first two decades of the 20th Century, the town had nowhere at all. Town Board minutes show them meeting in the offices of the town utility department – offices which they rented from local businessman M.L. Halferty.

Town Board members Carver, Gatwood and Moore agreed the best location was right beside the AFD's current one, so on May 14, 1930, days after the AFD's 42nd birthday, they advertised bids for "the general construction of a Fire Station and Town Building".

A New Deal project, designed to put people to work during the Great Depression, funded the building. The architect was A.M. Strauss of Fort Wayne. In June the Town Board granted contracts: Construction went to Hiatt Bros. of Albion, plumbing to P&H Co. of Albion, and heating to the Albion Hardware Co.

According to the *Albion New Era*, a fellow named Ernest Weeks purchased the old fire station, which had been not at the exact same spot but just south, between the new building and the property that would one day be the fourth fire station.

Weeks moved the old firehouse to his farm west of town, where it was undoubtedly fated to house hay, machinery, or animals. Put to pasture, so to speak, maybe with horses that once pulled the chemical engine.

Or maybe not. I've always wanted to own my own fire station; maybe Weeks painted an old pickup truck red, parked it in the retired firehouse, and made siren noises while no one was looking.

Apparently the old firehouse was too close to the new site to remain there during construction. That left the '29 in the Chevy garage, and maybe Chief Gatwood's other three units waited in garages and sheds of the volunteers; when a call came in, firefighters would race to the one closest to them.

Decades later, the 1929 engine spent several years in the garage of long time firefighter Phil Jacob – which gives a whole new slant to the old story about having no room in the garage for the family car. By then the old fire truck had been retired, but even though they had no room in the fire station, the volunteers couldn't bear to part with it.

(And no, nobody ever caught Phil sitting in his garage, making siren noises.)

The new fire station had a large apparatus room upstairs and more garage space in the basement, as well as office areas for town workers and a meeting room for the Town Board. The AFD once more had plenty of room in a new, modern firehouse, which would serve them for another thirty years.

Albion's 1930 fire station/town hall originally had two overhead doors, later combined into one. A fire siren towered above it, and the bell tower held, yes, a bell.

A Night at the Opera House

By 1931 the AFD had almost completely mechanized their firefighting fleet. The '29 became the lead unit, and the volunteers transferred the chemical engine's equipment to the bed of a Ford pickup truck. They tipped the newest hose cart, which held 350 feet of hose, with a trailer hitch that allowed the pickup or a volunteer's vehicle to tow it to a fire. The other hose cart, which now carried 200 feet of hose, stayed on a rarely utilized reserve status.

Chief Gatwood, two assistant chiefs, and eighteen volunteers now protected the 1,108 residents of Albion. That made up the AFD on January 16, 1931, when the Albion Opera House caught fire.

The opera house was and is a two story brick structure, near the middle of the block on the north side of the Courthouse square. Earlier that evening the American Legion put on a play upstairs, but as far as anyone knows the play's not the thing that started the blaze. The *Noble County Democrat* speculated that defective wiring, or perhaps a cigarette carelessly discarded by one of the play's cast members, may have been the cause.

The *Democrat* had a special interest in this particular fire: Its office occupied most of the lower floor, while the Noble County Abstract Co. took up the southwest corner.

Flames spread through the second floor until someone noticed them at around 11 p.m. Although many accounts of the fire and its aftermath survive, little is recorded of the fire department's strategy in fighting it. Still, we can make some conjectures:

The volunteers connected both engines to hydrants on the courthouse square. They managed to get into the first floor of the building, but heavy smoke and deteriorating conditions, which included the danger of roof collapse, soon drove them out. They set up defensive positions to protect other businesses, in a "surround and drown" operation. Most of the fire involved the roof area, but the firefighters had no aerial ladder and had to arc streams of water from the ground to reach over the walls.

By the time mutual aid fire departments arrived the chemical engine's water stream slowed to a trickle, as the unit ran out of chemicals. Both the hose carts went into operation, to supply hose from hydrants two to four blocks away.

Although the upstairs was gutted, firefighters managed to delay the blaze from dropping down into the first floor. As they fought the fire, others worked to salvage the downstairs contents, as the *Noble County Democrat* reported:

"It opened our eyes, wide, to the real greatness of courageous friendship when literally hundreds of men and boys braved the ever-menacing danger of a burning, crashing building to help us save as much as possible of our plant from that trembling structure."

Technical help came from the *Noble County Democrat's* mechanical department: "They labored fearlessly, intelligently and tirelessly in that darkened, smoke-filled room, rescuing with unerring skill such portions of the plant as could be removed, first giving careful attention to the seemingly hundreds of vital records, mailing lists and so forth. There was no running in useless circles. There wasn't a wasted step. Time counted and the boys knew it.

"They worked as if drilled especially for the tasks they performed. They systematically supervised the army of volunteer workers in the removal of approximately four thousand dollars' worth of type without the loss of a minute or an ounce of type, which in itself was a heretofore unheard of accomplishment. They … salvaged several thousands of dollars' worth of other material such as type cases, type cabinets and all light machinery that could be carried by manpower."

And so the *Noble County Democrat* could publish that account, just a week after the fire. Although flames didn't enter the first floor, the surround and drown operation caused much water and smoke damage, which crippled the printing operation. The paper instead took advantage of their salvaged equipment, and assistance offered by other area newspapers, to publish while repairs went on.

Albion's last hose cart left the hand-drawn age, then was towed behind a truck that carried the AFD's formerly horse-drawn chemical equipment, before being retired to parade duty.

Afterward, the abstract office moved to the Farmer's State Bank building. At the time, most thought the Albion Opera House would never be rebuilt – if used at all, the upper half would have to be razed, leaving a one story structure.

But by the first week in February reconstruction began, with men named Moore and Thomas employed to remodel the first floor. Twenty-seven local businessmen each donated $100 to rebuild the upper story, with a bigger stage and a new arched roof, and within two months the new opera house reopened.

To this day, in the hidden corners of the still standing opera house, one can see signs of fire and smoke damage – testament that, even then, America's firefighters could make a difference.

As for the *Noble County Democrat*, its office and printing plant moved to the J. Herbert Cockley store at 124 North Orange Street, which the editor identified as "commonly known as the Walters building". The print equipment was reconditioned, and prepared for use.

On Valentine's Day the *Noble County Democrat* showed off its new home at an open house, with the editor serving coffee and homemade doughnuts to the scores who attended. The *Noble County Democrat* later became the *Noble County American*, and remained in that building until they stopped publishing in the 1980s.

I wonder how many of Albion's senior citizens of 1931 still remembered the time before the AFD's founding forty-two years earlier, when the very idea of saving a burning building seemed pure fantasy.

The 1930 Albion Fire Station/Town Hall as it looked pretty much brand new, surrounded by some cool antique cars. Okay, maybe they weren't antique then … (Photo courtesy Old Jail Museum of Noble County.)

CHAPTER SIX

The 1930s:
Improvements and Retirement
Or,
Out With the Old, in With the Other Stuff

Aging equipment and a drive toward modernization caused many changes in the AFD's apparatus line-up over the next decade. The newest of the two hose carts was twenty years old, and since the pumper and the truck that carried the chemical engine now each held 450 feet of 2 ½ and 100 feet of 1 inch hose, the carts seemed unneeded.

Not long after the opera house fire, the AFD retired the older of the two carts. Somehow it found its way to the rural Albion barn of Leonard Summers, who according to the "Ghost Towns of Noble County" website (www.rootsweb.ancestry.com/~inncgs/ghosts.html), took over running the Bakertown store southeast of Albion in 1935. In 1969 Summers donated the apparatus to the Old Jail Museum in Albion.

By the late '30s the last hose cart was taken out of service, although the volunteers maintained it as a parade piece. For a time, it too rested at the Old Jail Museum, and passed into obscurity. You can imagine my reaction when I discovered both, along with an Avilla Fire Department hose cart, had been there all along: on the same property I toured several times as a child, and within a block of where the original fire station stood.

The restored unit has been returned to the firefighters' care, and rests in a town owned storage building along with other, much newer fire equipment.

Sometime between 1930 and 1937 John Gatwood, after presiding over the AFD's changeover to all gas powered apparatus, retired and turned his chief's helmet over to Harry Campbell. During Campbell's term, Albion would buy several new pieces of fire equipment, including an unprecedented innovation: the first "rural" truck.

Training? What's that?

Like water supply, firefighter training improved over the years. In 1888 a recruit picked up a hose or ax and went to work. He learned from his mistakes – if his mistakes didn't kill him. Of course, on the job experience wouldn't do much for buildings that burned while rookies got their bearings.

By the '30s, most fire departments held regular drills. They also had contests to teach basic firefighting skills, such as "waterball", and Albion volunteers attended regional fire schools.

AFD firefighters head into an inferno during a 2008 live fire exercise, thanks to a special trailer brought to Albion for training. It was the only trailer fire they ever liked.

The Indiana State Fire Marshall's office organized one such school, held in Kendallville in December, 1937. It featured talks on 12 subjects, highlighted by motion pictures "depicting effective fire prevention and fighting the element", as the *Kendallville News-Sun* put it. Training films were a big deal in 1937, two years before Hollywood's banner year of "The Wizard of Oz" and "Gone With the Wind". Volunteers attended from Albion, Avilla, Corunna, Kendallville, Rome City, Wolcottville, Howe, and LaGrange.

Training requirements have multiplied today, as the challenges of modern fire, rescue, hazardous material, and medical services increase. Firefighters are also required to have training certifications these days, so rookies tend to spend their first few years doing more training than anything else.

Don't Park There, Moron

Meanwhile, the Albion Town Board dealt with another problem related to fire protection. Sometimes it seems like whoever bought the first vehicle Ford ever made drove straight out and parked it in front of a fire hydrant.

Albion experienced the problem as much as any bigger city. Since a blocked hydrant was worthless, in November of 1937 a new ordinance took effect:

"No vehicle shall be parked within fifteen feet of any water plug, or so as to obstruct or hinder anyone from gaining access to such plug with fire apparatus and fire hose." ("Think before you park" should have done just fine.)

The term **plug** related to the original water mains installed on the east coast, which had no hydrants plumbed into them. To access the water, firefighters had to dig into the street, then drill a hole into the wooden mains. After the fire they – you guessed it – plugged them.

Blocking a hydrant seems like a pretty dumb idea even before it became illegal, but drivers searching for a spot on a crowded street have their minds elsewhere. Fire protection has never been a high priority for many people.

Out of Town ... What If?

Although no longer horse drawn, the chemical equipment was a quarter of a century old, outdated, and increasingly unreliable. If it ran out of chemicals or broke down the '29 engine would be left alone, and that unit often left town as rural calls for help increased.

At one time most rural homes were farmhouses; if one of them caught fire there was no way to call for help, let alone fight the blaze with hand drawn equipment. But more houses went up in the country, and telephone service spread to them. In August, 1938, for instance, the '29 left Albion three times in just one week.

Two of those calls were barn fires, one at the Oliver Strelby home in Jefferson Township, and another that leveled a large barn on the "old Gloyd farm, just south of Kimmel".

In the latter case the Albion, Ligonier, and, according to one newspaper, Kimmel fire departments could only wet down the nearby home and outbuildings.

A roof crew works on ventilation while another gains access through a window in this mid-80s rural fire, also in Jefferson Township, near Albion.

Kimmel no longer has a fire department – since I found no other mention of it, it's possible that it never did, and the newspaper made a mistake.

By far the most serious of the three fires started early on the morning of August 23, in the basement of a Rome City frame store building owned by W.A. Williams.

The Rome City Fire Department called out fire units from Albion, Kendallville, and Wolcottville to help, but by the time they arrived a second business had become involved. Firefighters concentrated their streams on neighboring structures as flames gutted two stores – a beer parlor and grocery store – for a $10,000 loss.

Albion citizens began to get concerned. When someone called for help they needed to send it, because a major structure fire in Albion would require the same help in return. But suppose a fire happened in Albion after the town's one engine left?

They became even more nervous after retiring the chemical engine in the late 30s. Since chemical power proved to be limited, few people were sorry to see it go. Still, it left all the fire department eggs in one basket – which is how they ended up with a chemical engine in the first place.

Besides, few emergencies bigger than a shed fire could be controlled with one fire engine. That meant more and more mutual aid calls, which left area communities without protection. Obviously, Albion needed two engines. As if the decision was that easy.

The Town Board wanted to know why they alone should pony up for a new engine, when its obvious use would be to protect homes in rural areas and other towns - where people didn't pay town taxes. At the time, the town of Albion funded all the fire department's equipment and upkeep, although on individual runs they billed other townships to defray operating costs.

The counter argument was that the new engine was to protect Albion itself: When one left town for fires, the other stayed behind. But to most it seemed reasonable to assume outlying areas should help pay for the new truck, so citizens began a fundraising effort to collect donations. As if to punctuate the work, a 1938 disaster gave brutal reminder of why they needed to make the effort.

Albion Hardware Burns

Like many such fires, the one that destroyed the Albion Hardware started at night; it was discovered just after 1 a.m. on Monday, October 17. Men clung to the 29's rear and back steps as the lone fire truck answered the fire whistle's shrill call.

The blaze started in the basement but, according to the *Albion New Era,* building owners Himes and Neidhardt had no idea how: "The basement was cleaned last week and the light switch at the door was shut off when they left the store, so they are sure it could not have started from defective wiring."

The building had an elevator, and the blaze spread up the shaft to involve both floors. Firefighters called for help from Kendallville and Ligonier, and each town sent a truck to assist. Together, the crews of the three engines managed to keep the flames from spreading north to the Kroger store or south to the post office, although each exposed business suffered smoke and water damage.

After the fire, the post office moved temporarily "to the I.O.O.F. room formerly occupied by the A&P Store". So, for a short time, Albion had an I.O.O.F.A.P.P.O.

The *Albion New Era* summed up the possibilities: "With a high wind, a scarcity of water and without the assistance of our neighbor's fire trucks, the entire block might have been wiped out."

As if the regular hazards weren't bad enough! But the editor was right: The burned building was repaired and remodeled, and after being restocked the store opened for business.

Engine '39

The hardware store fire gave new emphasis to fundraising efforts, as Albionites considered what might have happened had the '29 been out on another call at the time. And again, if so many fires required more than one engine to be brought under control, why did Albion have only one? An *Albion New Era* article summed up the situation as of December 7, 1938:

"The chassis for the new rural fire truck, to be housed in Albion and operated by the local fire department, has been delivered to the fire

The '39 fire engine backs into the firehouse after returning from a call, in a still from a film taken in the late 40s or early 50s. (Still photo from a video courtesy Bill Shultz and the Noble County Historical Society.)

equipment factory, and will be delivered in Albion within a few weeks. After the delivery of this fire truck it will no longer be necessary for the town's truck to answer rural calls and leave the town unprotected during its absence, a matter to be greatly appreciated by all.

"A portion of the funds for the purchase of a new truck is being raised by subscription and as the party doing the subscription work is confined to his home by illness, it would be appreciated if those not already seen and wishing to contribute, especially those having property in Albion township outside the town of Albion, who should no longer expect the taxpayers of the town of Albion to furnish them fire protection gratis, would call at the Bank and leave their subscription."

Subtle, much? But point taken, and supporters gathered enough to pay for the new apparatus that arrived at about the same time Adolf Hitler was casting a greedy eye around Europe. I assume the two events weren't related.

The 1939 engine's 350 gpm pump made it a little more powerful than the 29's. In another way it was very unusual: While the typical fire pump was mounted near the middle of the truck, this one went over the front bumper. That engineering allowed the pump, unlike that of the '29, to be engaged while the truck stayed in motion.

This **pump and roll** ability wasn't needed in town, but it came in handy with field and wildland fires, which often spread over large areas but could be controlled with relatively small amounts of water. A firefighter with the nozzle of a one inch booster hose could stay on the truck and knock down the flames while the driver circled the fire.

Although it was a great improvement in fighting ground cover fires, the new truck didn't make all that much difference for rural structure fires. It carried no more on-board water than the '29, and still had to find a pond or stream to continue once the booster tank emptied.

Another decade would pass before the concept of fire department tankers began to gain popularity in the area. The idea of separate apparatus for town and rural fires, however, became established. To this day some fire departments operate divided equipment inventories: some trucks sent only to rural fires, some not allowed to leave town limits at all.

Fire Death

Although a blaze in March, 1939, caused little property damage, it provided a horrifying reminder of the danger to lives.

Mrs. Rosenia Kuhns was still on the mend from burns received a year earlier, when her clothes caught fire while she cooked at her kitchen stove. At 77, Mrs. Kuhns, reputed to be the stepmother of Noble County's notorious outlaw Marvin Kuhns, had been blind for 15 years.

Her brother, Charles Rosenogle, left her in a home on North Elm Street while he ran an errand, and returned ten minutes later to the smell of smoke. He found Rosenia Kuhns on the floor, "her clothing burned off and her entire body terribly burned", according to the *Albion New Era's* obituary.

"It was first believed embers from her pipe set her clothing on fire, but the opinion of Coroner Myron C. Hutchins of Kendallville is that a match with which she was relighting the pipe caused the tragedy."

This revealed the danger of smoking in a much more horrible way than any label on a cigarette package.

The home was not badly damaged, and firefighters could do nothing to help the elderly woman. Unfortunately, this would not be Albion's last experience with a fire related death.

Close Call

A fire that broke out soon after caused no serious property damage, but had the potential for disaster. Any lumber mill has large amounts of exposed flammable materials, and the potential for rapid fire spread and radiant heat. The fire at the Chilcote-Kitt Lumber Mill started in a pile of shavings, and burned a hole in the floor near the wall by the time fire units arrived.

(Notice I said units, plural. The '39 may have been meant for rural use, but when somebody yells that a lumber mill is on fire, the volunteers will play it safe and empty the station.)

Whether because of prompt response or sheer luck, firefighters knocked the flames down before major damage resulted. Satisfied volunteers marked it as a "save". The number of saves would increase over time.

Even doubling fire protection doesn't guarantee a prompt response to every call. For example, on a Tuesday morning in August, 1939, the nightmare of small town firefighters came true when two blazes broke out at the same time. The incident typified the two types that took volunteers away from their home towns: rural fires, and blazes in other communities.

Both broke out around 1:30 a.m., but Rome City's call for help got to Albion first. A lamp ignited a curtain at Sylvan Lake, and within minutes one of the closely packed cottages became a torch. By the time mutual aid arrived from Albion, Wolcottville and Kendallville, four cottages blazed, while flames spread to two others.

With plenty of water available from the lake, firefighters managed to control the flames after a hard, three hour fight. Although the two exposed cottages sustained damage, the firefighters saved them, and protected other nearby structures.

Meanwhile, a "well filled" barn at the Bert Buckles farm, southeast of Ligonier, burst into flames. Well filled with what? Hay or straw bales, one would assume, which provided plenty of fuel to turn a large wooden building into a torch. Since the Ligonier Fire Department was busy with units from Topeka and Goshen at still a third blaze, which consumed a hardware and general store at Millersburg in a neighboring county, a call went out to Albion.

To coin a phrase, when it rains, it pours. I didn't really coin that phrase.

According to the *Albion New Era*, "The Albion fire company was called, but was unable to reach the Buckles farm as they were in Rome City." The article gave no further information.

It's unlikely that Chief Campbell allowed both Albion engines to go to Rome City. It could be all the available volunteers – they numbered about 20 at this time – went with the '39 in Rome City, leaving no one around to man the '29 for the second call. A more likely explanation is the town fathers refused to allow the '29 to leave town – and the night's events would tend to reinforce their caution. If three fires could break out at the same time, why not four – in the courthouse, perhaps, or the Albion school?

Again, to this day some fire departments refuse to allow their "city" trucks to leave town, no matter how bad the situation outside corporate limits.

In any case, sending an Albion truck to a barn fire so far out of town would have been futile. They simply had no water; not even enough to protect exposures, if the exposures happened to be close to the main fire.

Even with its small water tank, the '39 successfully doused some rural fires without depleting Albion's fire protection. Few complained about continued high fire losses in the country, because rural homeowners and farmers accepted for decades that if a fire broke out, no one could hope to stop it.

For the next dozen years the status quo held, with the two engines being Albion's only fire apparatus.

A wall collapses during a training fire. This home originally burned on a day so hot that fire hose stuck to the melted asphalt pavement.

CHAPTER SEVEN

The 1940s:
Because that's the way we've always done it

Periods of growth that marked the AFD's history vanished during the 40s. There was little innovation or new equipment, and no new apparatus. What was there? World War II.

Fire equipment manufacturers retooled their factories to support the war effort, raw materials were in short supply, and the little equipment still being made got sent to areas that badly needed new trucks and gear, such as London.

The unusual fire threats caused by World War II produced new methods to fight and prevent fires, but those ideas wouldn't filter down to small town fire departments for many years.

During the war things stayed quiet in Albion, but Albionites had only to look to Kendallville for reminders to stay ready. Five major fires struck that city in the mid-forties, four of them in a

Big fires, like this one that destroyed Albion's feed mill, seem far too regular for any small town. Here radiant heat sets fire to a utility pole and electric wires. Shocking.

six month period from mid-1945 to January, 1946. All hit businesses on Main Street, burning a cigar store, a grocery, the Mary Jane Shop, and the "Lang Block on South Main", as well as a room in the block where the *Kendallville News-Sun* newspaper operated.

No, I'm not certain what a Mary Jane Shop was … but Mary Jane must have been popular. (It was a clothing or shoe store, get your mind out of the gutter.)

After the war's end, fortunes turned for the worse in Albion. Fires there were not so major as the ones in Kendallville, but bad enough to those who suffered through them.

A blizzard struck the area in February, 1946 with heavy snow blown about by a 35 mph wind. On the Thursday before the storm hit, the temperature dropped in the afternoon from 34 degrees to 2 below zero.

Firefighters everywhere know they'll be called out in the worst possible weather, so Albion's crew couldn't have been surprised when the fire whistle went off at about 2:30 a.m. Friday. An overheated furnace started the fire at the Elvin Bradigan home, and the family of six awoke to find thick smoke filling their house. Still clad in night clothes, they got out but narrowly avoided suffocation.

Ed Hines, a neighbor whose home stood 20 feet away, turned in the alarm. The firefighters forced their way through snow drifts in sub-zero weather to find the wind whipping flames through the structure and endangering the Hines home. There was no chance to salvage belongings.

Assisted by a unit from Kendallville, the firefighters managed to save the Hines home, despite its proximity to the fire. The Hines family published their thanks in the next issue of the local newspapers.

Slow Weeks, Busy Days

In small towns, weeks – sometimes months – go by without a fire call. While this is nothing to complain about, it makes firefighters nervous. Tradition has it that the next fire after a dry spell will be "The Big One", and the number of minor calls, such as medical assists, accidents, and alarms, was smaller back then. When a call finally came in hearts raced, adrenalin rushed, and the volunteers dropped everything to run – perhaps a bit faster than usual – for the station.

On the other hand, remember the grocer's maxim: All the shoppers will try to check out at the same time. In the fire service, that meant some days when the whole town seemed to burn, bit by bit. An article in the March 27, 1946 *Albion New Era* described one such day:

"The Albion Fire Department was called to the Eva Jaquay property, occupied by Lawrence Davis, to extinguish a small blaze Saturday afternoon. A few minutes later they extinguished a fire in the car of Archie Pippenger parked on the street. Then they got called to the east side of the court house to put out a blazing Model A car belonging to Mrs. Bessie Moore. This car was badly damaged."

They say bad news comes in threes. At a time when the monthly run total for Albion sometimes totaled zero, that was a pretty big day.

As can be seen, automobiles and other gasoline powered vehicles greatly increased the AFD's activities when they came into general use. This is one area in which the term "business is booming" isn't a good thing.

April Fools

Sometimes people forget volunteers must be ready *always*; there's no time when a fire isn't possible. Sometimes even firefighters forget that.

On April first, 1946, the AFD held its traditional fish fry at the fire station. Unlike today, the fish fry wasn't a fundraiser, but a social event held on a Monday before the regular fire meeting, with the Town Board members as guests.

Chief Harry Campbell himself caught the fish – one of his more pleasant duties – and they were prepared and served by firefighters Ted Frymier, Byron and Welty Smith, Harry Butler, and Don Barcus, at "Gerald Fryonler's restaurant". In the midst of their supper, a young girl ran into the establishment and reported a vehicle fire at the REMC, which at the time was around the corner on East Main Street.

(The REMC – Rural Electric Membership Corporation – was at the time in the same building that, back when it was a Chevy garage, first housed the '29 engine.)

The men can't be blamed for the obvious conclusion: It was an April Fool's joke. Certain their falling for the joke gave some prankster great amusement, the volunteers hurried to the scene.

There they found a car, blazing merrily away.

AFD Fire Prevention officer Phil Jacob at the wheel of the restored '29 in the 2011 Chain O' Lakes Festival Parade, with retired chief Jim Applegate along for the ride. The 21st Century AFD command vehicle tails them.

Maybe they still laughed when they returned to finish their meal, but from then on they took every alarm a bit more seriously.

Happy Centennial – Let's Not Do It Again, Sometime

If the organizers of Albion's centennial celebration promised a hot time, they wished they'd used a different phrase by the time the day ended.

In October, 1946, the town of Albion threw itself a one hundredth birthday party, complete with a carnival and a Ferris Wheel. A newspaper article describes the AFD's unintentional part in providing entertainment:

"The gasoline motor used in operating the Ferris wheel at the centennial celebration caught fire and created considerable excitement among the crowd, and caused much flurry among those aboard the wheel.

"Quick work on the part of the fire department averted serious damage. Persons on the wheel were removed without injury. Much courage was shown by some of the youngsters aboard the wheel at the time. A farm tractor was pressed into service to operate the wheel.

"The fire was barely extinguished when the department was called to the Skinner Lake Conservation Club property, two miles east of Skinner Lake on State Road 8. Fire was confined to a woodshed containing corn cobs to be used for fuel. Grass fires also called out the fire department during the Centennial."

How many grass fires? Probably a rash of them, and "rash" is a good description considering their annoyance and spread factors.

Notice most of those calls didn't directly relate to the centennial, but happened on that day anyway. This kind of thing is a well-documented reality, but also a mystery, like full moons and Herbert Hoover's economic policy.

Although the 40s generally stayed quiet, 1946 stayed an unusually active year. AFD members finished it up in December, when fire broke out at the Ackerman Mercantile Building. Instead of the typical early morning fire, this blaze started at 2:30 in the afternoon, and a large crowd braved the cold to watch the extinguishment efforts.

Firefighters arrived to see heavy smoke push from the rear of the building, as fire involved the ceiling area. The volunteers crawled through the smoke, and managed to extinguish the blaze before flames spread through the rest of the structure. Final damage estimates amounted to less than $300, and soon the store went back to business.

As they took up their hose and returned to the station to melt ice from their clothes and equipment, the volunteers must have taken great satisfaction in knowing they'd chalked up another "save".

CHAPTER EIGHT

The 1950s:
Rural Fire Protection
Or:
Water, Water, Nowhere

In the early 50s Albion firefighters received their first "pay raise", an increase of compensation from 50 cents to 1 dollar for every hour on a call. The money is considered compensation, rather than pay (for fuel, clothing lost to smoke or sparks, time spent … maybe aspirin, stress, bandages), so technically they remain volunteers.

1952 brought major changes to the AFD. After 15 years as chief, Harry Campbell reached mandatory retirement age and stepped down, to be replaced by Byron K. Smith. The *Albion New Era* praised the retiring chief's service: "Harry deserves the highest commendation from the town folks for his splendid leadership and efforts as our fire chief … he was always on the job and ready for action whenever fire threatened our homes or business places … so many thanks Harry, for a fine job."

Town and Country

Before retiring, Campbell started work toward the AFD's next apparatus purchase, a job completed by Smith. The '29 was now over 20 years old, and the men were no doubt tired of being frozen in the winter and soaked by summer rains in a truck with no cab roof.

They faced a duel problem: Neither of Albion's trucks had the pumping capacity to protect a growing town, but at the same time neither had a water tank large enough for rural structure fires. The '39 had been purchased as a rural engine, but other than its ability to pump and roll, it had no real advantage.

So the town needed a truck that could both pump more water, *and* carry more water. And couldn't there be some better, more efficient way of putting water on the fire, so it wouldn't take so much to put it out?

Fire Doesn't Wait

Fires don't wait for someone to decide on a better way to fight them. On a Wednesday afternoon in January, 1952, a truck caught fire inside the Noble County Highway garage. Hap Jaquay reached through the flames and smoke to release the truck's brakes, and garage employees pushed it outside.

The truck, a 1950 model, must have been unlucky, because at the time of the fire it awaited repairs after being in an accident the summer before. This time, its case was terminal.

The highway workers acted quickly and prevented the building from catching fire. Maybe they remembered a similar fire on April 11, 1945, which destroyed the highway garage and much of its equipment at the former location, on South York Street (right next to the *Albion New Era* office).

The next morning a fire broke out in, of all places, a water pump house. The Noble County Home, also known as the poor farm or infirmary, was located in a large brick building northwest of Albion. Because of its size and occupancy, the Albion volunteers worried about fire breaking out in the home itself – but never in its pump house, a brick and frame building measuring 20 by 22 feet.

The '39's crew came out at 10:30 in the morning and arrived to find the contents of the pump house, including a large electric motor and a garden tractor, blazing. They called the Ligonier Fire Dept. to help, and the two forces controlled the blaze before the home itself sustained any damage.

A water pump fire may be a funny idea, but the volunteers didn't laugh. They saw yet another example that *any* building, no matter how unlikely or "fire proof", could catch fire.

Trustees of the townships around Albion heard of the pump house fire, and thought of the much larger building right beside it. They saw an increasing number of structures built with no nearby water source.

So, in early 1952, the political leaders of four townships and the town of Albion did something rare: They all agreed. The townships would purchase a new fire truck, and the town would house and man it.

On February 13, 1952, the trustees of four townships gathered: Lloyd Cole of Albion Township, Ray Hanlon of York Township, William Duesler of Jefferson Township, and Franklin Geiger of Green Township. They jointly advertised bids for "equipment suitable for the rural fire fighting purposes of said townships". All townships would pay an equal share toward the truck except for Green, which would pay a half share. (From that time to this, Albion provided protection for Green Township's northern half, and Churubusco protected its southern half.)

Welcome to Modern Technology

The legendary American LaFrance company built the truck on a Ford chassis, and word of its purchase resulted in front page articles in the local papers. The March 19 issue of the *Albion New Era* noted the cooperation between the townships, the Albion Chamber of Commerce, the fire department, and the Town Board. As a group, everyone felt they got the "most for their money" – $15,000, which today wouldn't even buy the equipment for a fire engine, let alone the truck itself.

"At the present time", the *Albion New Era* commented, "all that is available locally is the 1929 truck bought by the Albion town years ago, and the 1939 truck bought by popular subscription by residents of York and Jefferson townships and others. It is wonderful to see how well the Albion volunteers are able to fight a fire with this antiquated equipment. It is a fine thing that they will have so much more to work with."

It wouldn't be the last time Albion worked with "antiquated" fire equipment. In fact, the fantastic modern technology on board the 1952 pumper would stay in service for the next four decades.

For its time the '52 was, indeed, the best rural fire engine available, and at 500 gpm its pumping capacity came close to the other two pumpers combined. The same went for the water tank, which held an impressive 500 gallons. Pneumonia and hypothermia beware – it had a fully enclosed cab.

Compared to the 450 feet of hose carried on the other two engines, the '52 came with 1,000 feet of 2 ½ inch diameter hose, plus 400 feet of 1 ½ hose. The smaller hoseline delivered less water, but could be more easily maneuvered during an interior fire attack.

The new fire engine also came equipped with an **auxiliary pump** (now called a portable pump), which could be carried to ponds and streams the truck couldn't reach, ensuring a continuous water supply.

The 1952 engine, retired after four decades, rests behind the fire station. Ironically, the location here is between the town's third and fourth fire stations -- and on the very spot where the second station once stood.

It also carried a portable generator, then called an "auxiliary light plant", powerful enough to "run the Albion (medical) clinic except for the X-ray machine, if the power went off in an emergency". It could power flood lights at the scene of a fire.

Still another new piece of equipment was a **resuscitator**, which began the AFD's involvement in the emergency medical service. The device forced oxygen into the lungs of accident or illness victims, hopefully keeping them alive until they could be delivered to a hospital. It could do the same for firefighters suffering from smoke inhalation.

But in the most important innovation, as far as rural property owners were concerned, "the new truck will carry … a special high pressure nozzle for the new type fog style spray, that is proving so effective and also takes such a small amount of water. The water becomes almost a vapor with this spray and often times, according to those who have seen it used, does more good in putting out a fire than huge quantities of water poured on directly. This is particularly a good idea in rural communities where large amounts of water are not available.

"This will mean 95 percent of Albion's fires can be put out with less than 100 gallons of water, we were told by a man who knows as much about firefighting as almost anyone in Albion." (No, I don't know who that man was, but he'd just about have to be one of the volunteers.)

The system relied only partly on the pump, which had two settings: capacity, which pumped the full 500 gpm; and pressure, which pumped half the capacity, at twice the pressure. These **"two stage" pumps** remained common across the country in the latter half of the 20th Century.

For the actual "high pressure", the pump would be set at pressure, and the water pumped through the two one inch "booster" lines mounted on reels above the pump. The lines were tipped with special nozzles, which made the water come out in a fog of tiny droplets, under high pressure.

In theory the fine droplets of water absorb more heat than a solid stream, because more of the water's surface area is exposed to the heat of the flames. The water absorbs the heat and turns to steam, which expands to many times its original volume and suffocates the fire. So a high pressure fog nozzle, dispensing a few gallons per minute, should douse a fire much faster than a regular nozzle spray of well over 150 gpm.

Just one little problem: It didn't work.

Fog was, indeed, the most efficient way to absorb heat, but the high pressure nozzles didn't provide enough volume. A few gallons per minute won't absorb as much heat as large fires generate no matter how it's delivered, so the fire simply wouldn't go out unless small to begin with. Today's nozzles, which deliver large amounts of water on a spray setting, can absorb heat the way the high pressure nozzles were advertised to. Even that's less popular as time goes by, because the aggressive firefighters of today sometimes lose their visibility and get burned from the sudden clouds of steam.

Not that it ever happened to this author. Nope. By the way, steam burns really hurt.

This would all be learned later, through bitter experience, and it had nothing to do with the excellent design of the truck itself. Although the high pressure fog concept proved unsuccessful, central Noble County still got a major improvement in fire protection.

It's a Beauty, eh?

In early August, 1952, workers unloaded the new engine from a railroad car, and the firefighters went to work testing it out.

A plan had been made for residents of the townships to receive firefighting training and assist whenever a fire broke out in their area, but there's no record that large numbers of rural residents joined the department at the time. In actual practice it would have been difficult because they had no radio pagers, and lived too far from town to hear the large siren placed over the fire station.

Along with their description of the new fire engine, the *Albion New Era* published a list of all the volunteer firefighters as of 1952:

"Chief Byron Smith, John Beckley (secretary), Bob Beckley, Dale Guthrie, Chuck Mendenhall, Lauren Smith, Jay Davis, Peck Campbell, Max Sorgenfrei, Jim Girard, Joe Steel, Bob Magnuson, Buck Seymoure, Bob Berkes, Ted Frymier, Harry Metz, Martin Kitt, and Jim Applegate. Several of the men who had been on the force for many years have retired recently and will serve in an advisory capacity when needed." (Remember, they had a mandatory retirement age at the time.)

When the engine arrived, a picture of it published in the *Noble County American* showed it came with no revolving red light on the cab. It could be the top light made the truck too high to fit on the railroad car, and so had to be mounted after delivery, or maybe the truck relied on its siren to alert traffic to its approach. In either case, later a red light was mounted, and today no one can imagine a fire truck without a complement of warning lights.

The *Albion New Era* was impressed: "The new fire truck for Albion is a real sensation … the volunteer firemen have been busy testing it out and learning all of the many features which will make it important to the fire safety of the community … its shiny red finish and all the interesting coils of hose and brass equipment certainly make you envy the firemen who have been guarding our community from fire … while the firemen aren't looking for a fire, they certainly are getting as big a thrill out of the new truck as the rest of us are."

Morbid as it sounds, many of the firefighters probably *did* hope for a fire, although they'd never admit it – even to themselves. They were men of action, ready to test their new truck in a real fire.

Drought

Superstition has it that big fires always come before a new truck is delivered, and a fire drought follows. That was the case in 1952. Plenty of calls came in for the rest of the year and the next – in fact, more than usual because of a real drought, the weather kind – but no major ones.

A Salvation Army truck burned in Albion on October 10, possibly the 52's first call to service. Any of the three engines could handle a vehicle fire, but there's no doubt which one went. After that came minor runs like grass fires, and plenty of them.

Spring is the busy season for wildland fires in northern Indiana, but in 1952 a drought continued on into the fall. On October 25, a Sunday, *seven* grass fires broke out in one day, in addition to another the day before. On December 3rd the *Albion New Era* reported:

'The Albion Fire Department has been plenty busy. With brush fires owing to the drought and a nocturnal fire Sunday night around midnight, the department has really put in several hard weeks. We always owe a deep debt of gratitude for the willingness and response of the department to calls at any time of the day or night, and in any kind of weather."

Nothing else was recorded about the "nocturnal fire", except it happened at the Ernest Weeks property. However, you might remember Ernest Weeks is the man who bought the second Albion firehouse, when the town hall was built in 1930, and had it moved out to his farm. You can see the irony if what burned was that firehouse, which at the time would have been half a century old and probably looked like nothing more than a large wooden garage.

Dry weather lasted on into October of 1953, when an *Albion New Era* story tells of numerous fires due to the drought. The same story, by the way, mentions the purchase of brand new uniforms for the volunteers from Black's Mercantile Co., along with badges and hats. The men wanted to look as good at parades and other functions as their new truck did.

The '39 was still the truck of choice for grass fires because of its "pump and roll" capability. But with as many as seven fires reported in one day, sometimes more than one call came in at the same time. Then the '52 rolled while the '29 stayed in reserve. On days that busy, it didn't take long for firefighters to see the usefulness of having three trucks on hand.

Even with structure fires, two engines could control 95% of Albion's incidents. The third could join them on major fires, replace a truck down for repairs, training or maintenance, or handle a second call at the same time.

Because of those advantages, from then on AFD members tried to keep three fire engines in the inventory at all times.

Bring Your Own Water

It didn't take long for the volunteers to become disenchanted with their high pressure fog, just as the firefighters of 1914 discovered shortcomings in their chemical engine. But, while high pressure fog didn't work well on large fires, there still wasn't enough water at rural fire scenes to try more conventional methods.

The concept of water tankers (called "tenders" in the western U.S.) soon gained popularity in the area. It seemed the obvious solution: If you couldn't find enough water at the fire scene, bring your own!

The members decided to try it, and obtained a 1951 GMC truck, which had mounted on its back a 1,000 gallon water tank. (Until 2005 all AFD tankers were, as car salesmen say, pre-owned, having lived former lives as fuel or milk trucks.) Between the tanker and the '52 pumper, 1,500 gallons of water could be trucked to the scene, five times the amount carried before 1952.

1,500 gallons really wasn't so much – the '29 could pump it out in five minutes. But sometimes just enough water, if applied at the right time and place, could save a home. When that didn't work, the water could still protect other buildings that would have burned before, like the A.E. Jones farm leveled in 1929.

Firefighters build a 4,000 gallon tanker, the AFD's largest so far (since replaced by a 3,500 gallon truck). For decades every AFD tanker, rescue truck, and brush truck was a civilian vehicle remade from scratch into an emergency unit. That's the '29 in the lower left corner.

CHAPTER NINE

Modern Challenges
Or,
Well, They Were Modern Then ...

After two years as chief, Byron K. Smith was replaced in 1954 by Harry Metz, who guided the AFD through the rest of the 50s.

One more vehicles came in that decade. Although the '52 pumper carried a portable generator, fears of a major power outage and the need to fully illuminate a fire scene led to the purchase of a larger, more powerful "light plant". This generator was mounted on the bed of a 1949 Chevy pickup, which served for over a dozen years as the AFD's utility vehicle. In the fire service, utility vehicles would gradually evolve into rescue trucks.

Hello? Hello?

New advances in communication arrived in the 50s. By then most people had a telephone, so in 1958 a new system was set up to alert the volunteers of a run. When someone called the fire emergency number, phones in all the volunteer's homes would continuously ring, and go on ringing even after other firefighters picked up their receivers. That way everyone at home could be alerted. The first volunteer to reach the station would switch on the siren, so firefighters who weren't near their homes would also know to respond.

As this would affect the families of the volunteers – and an unhappy wife is an unhappy household – the families held a meeting in November to talk over the new telephone setup. Although the response wasn't recorded, it can be assumed some members of the household didn't like the idea. Still, spouses were used to the drawbacks that go with marrying a volunteer firefighter, and accepted late night phone calls as still another one.

A new radio base station was installed in the fire station at the same time as the fire siren. The '52 engine was equipped with the department's first mobile radio, and over the years those units became standard on every Albion fire truck. The ability of firefighters to communicate at the scene, as well as while enroute to a fire, increased immensely.

Milk Run and Other Hazards

Meanwhile the calls continued, although some turned out to be less serious than others. On June 16, 1956, a truck's brakes failed and it turned over at Skinner Lake, on the highway in front of Sam McColly's residence. The driver escaped injury, but the truck's load spilled out over the road – which is how many hazardous material incidents begin.

Yes, milk can be considered a hazardous material, if it's spilled into a waterway: It turns out some aquatic life is lactose intolerant. (Who do you suppose figured that one out?) In this case they could have left the milk to please neighborhood cats, but after awhile the smell would have been less than pleasant. Instead of crying over spilt milk three volunteers took a truck out to wash the liquid away. Where it got washed to wasn't reported, but they say the fishing's still good in Skinner Lake.

A much more serious incident involving a truck took place two days later, two and a half miles west of Kendallville on US Highway 6. (US 6, the Grand Army of the Republic Highway, is a sister highway to the more famous Route 66, and like it runs most of the nation's length.)

At 5 a.m. a semi-trailer loaded with 32,000 pounds of rubber caught fire, and the Kendallville Fire Department called for Albion's "water truck" to assist in dousing the blaze. Later that day the AFD caught its own call, a barn fire three miles west of town.

Almost everyone burned their trash those days, not only homeowners but area dumps, so it's little wonder so many fires originated there. In September, 1956, the AFD responded to a blaze at the Kimmell dump, and the same day extinguished a trash fire that spread to the roof of the Elmo Mfg. Co., on South Street in Albion.

"Controlled" burns have a bad habit of becoming less than controlled. Railroad crews would toss out flares to burn off grass, brush and old ties along their right of way, but they seldom stuck around to make sure the fire didn't get out of hand. Even if it didn't at first, the next train to go by often fanned flames onto nearby properties.

In November, 1956, a fire set by B&O Railroad workers spread through a woods, crossed a cornfield, and damaged a barn. Following standard procedure, the AFD sent the railroad company a bill for the response. Over the next four months, four bills and a letter went out, until B&O finally paid. For many, many years, relations between railroad companies and the fire departments their tracks passed near remained less than cordial.

Safety? We don't need no stinkin' safety!

The innovations kept on coming as fire departments tried to improve their service. Safety, unfortunately, stood low on the list of many firefighters. They held a widespread belief that the job would always be dangerous, a risk firefighters accepted, and many of them accepted it as a badge of honor. But improvements did come, if slowly.

For instance, each firefighter in Albion had a blue warning light for their personal vehicle, to alert other motorists when they responded to a fire call. Although the light doesn't permit volunteers to break traffic laws, it does allow them to alert other drivers and ask for the right of way. With some exceptions, those drivers who pay

Decades after air packs allowed firefighters to breathe in a hazardous atmosphere, thermal imaging units allow let them see through darkness and smoke. The firefighter on the right added to his team's safety with a portable radio in his coat pocket.

attention try to make room.

In 1957, Albion firefighters obtained an invention that revolutionized the fire service. Named at the time a "gas mask", the Self-Contained Breathing Apparatus (**SCBA**), is most often called an **air pack**. They were primitive compared to those in use today, but still a major improvement. Turns out breathing is good for your health.

Before, when firefighters had to enter a burning structure to make a rescue or fire attack, they had no more protection from toxic smoke and lack of oxygen than any civilian. In the 1800s some firefighters grew long beards: They would soak them with water, stuff them in their mouths and go in, hoping the wet hair would filter out the smoke.

While beards may filter out some smoke particles, they would be useless against low oxygen levels and toxic gas, and probably not all that popular with the ladies.

A firefighter who could take a few minutes inside before he collapsed was called "leather lunged" – which is a pretty good description of what their lungs looked like after a few years of such punishment. He would crawl on his belly, nose to the floor, and with luck stumble out a short time later to be replaced by another man. There are accounts of single fires in New York City in which hundreds of firefighters had to be treated for smoke inhalation.

A firefighter's worth as a "smoke eater" depended on how much of a "dose" he could take. Not all such firefighters passed away of cancer and lung diseases: Some died much more quickly, after inhaling too many toxins.

Gas masks filtered out smoke particles and some gases, but didn't provide oxygen. A fire has to breathe, just like a human, and often consumes the available oxygen in a burning enclosure. The SCBA provides tanks of compressed air to be strapped on the firefighters' backs. The air – not pure oxygen, something you don't want near a fire – is delivered into a mask to protect the face and eyes, as well as lungs.

The steel tanks were heavy, the air lasted only about 20 minutes, and the SCBA regulator tended to freeze up and malfunction in cold weather. (Not that such a thing ever happened to this author. But if it did, he'd have panicked when the air flow suddenly stopped.) But it beat the heck out of sucking smoke. Each new model since has been lighter and more comfortable to wear – relatively speaking – and the newest provide up to an hour of fresh air.

Some firefighters have ended up with chronic, lifelong back pain just from wearing those steel tanks for too long. Again, not that such a thing ever happened to this author. Ibuprofen is my friend.

Albion's volunteers didn't have to wait long to test their new devices. A fire in Minnie Herendeen's residence on South Street broke out February 1st, 1957. Thick smoke filled the 2 ½ story home, so firefighters chopped a hole in the roof to let the superheated smoke and gasses out.

That often misunderstood action – **roof ventilation** – helps prevent backdrafts and flashovers. A **backdraft** happens after a fire uses up all the oxygen in an area, then sucks in a fresh supply when a window is broken or door opened. Also called a smoke explosion, backdrafts have killed and injured many firefighters.

A **flashover** is much more common, and happens when all the materials in an area reach their ignition temperature at the same time, creating a ball of fire. Similar effects sometimes happen at alcohol-fueled family reunions.

Even quick roof ventilation rarely clears all smoke from a home, and in the case of the Herendeen incident, a smoky fire smoldered in hidden spaces along the attic and walls. The men could breathe with their masks, but heavy damage resulted because they still couldn't see through the smoke, and had trouble finding the exact location of the fire. It would be another half century before thermal imaging cameras helped solve the problem.

Historical Oops

The next time AFD personnel got called to a fire, air packs couldn't help – the building was doomed before they even reached the scene.

The Ligonier Fire Department responded first, when fire broke out in a two story frame dwelling in Wawaka on February 15. The occupants, Mr. and Mrs. Maurice Kinnison and their three children, got out safely, but by the time fire units arrived flames engulfed the century old home. Albion's tanker, and later the '52 pumper, came to help … but Wawaka is ten miles from the nearest firehouse, and has no hydrant system.

According to Wawaka legend, the first child born in Elkhart Township entered the world in that 100 year old home. This fire, then, can be seen as an historical disaster, but the more tragic aspect remains the fact that five people lost everything they owned.

Sparks and – Snow

Exactly one month later, a barn six miles south of Albion burned in a high wind, despite efforts of Albion, Wolf Lake and Churubusco firefighters. There's no record of how this fire started, but since the next day three grass fires broke out, a grass or trash fire is suspected.

One of those grass fires started from sparks blown out of the Albion dump, which spread to the DX bulk plant (later the Moorhouse bulk plant) at the corner of York and Railroad Streets. No damage resulted, but fire so near the complex of fuel tanks must have caused quite a scare. Sparks from the town dump started another grass fire in the same area that July.

Long after the town dump was closed, the land was turned into a mobile home park (where this author lived, for a time) that recorded at least one mobile home fire.

The 1957 grass fire season was interrupted the morning of May 8, when over ten inches of snow fell. The spring blizzard also interrupted the AFD's monthly "practice", when the trucks were driven and tested to ensure operation condition. Sometimes you have to drive in snow; sometimes you don't.

Cold Weather Fires

One of the most serious fires of 1957 occurred late in the year on Ben Edsall's property near town, when a large chicken house caught fire. The '52 pumper and the tanker headed out, joined by the '39 pumper and the utility truck along with 15 of the 18 volunteers, but by the time they arrived the large building blazed fiercely.

Units from Kendallville and Wolf Lake came to assist, and Albion's tanker hauled eight loads of water from town as the firefighters battled the flames for six hours, but no one could save the wooden structure or the 1,900 chickens inside. An unlimited supply of water would make little difference.

1958 didn't start off much better, with a house fire, two chimney fires, and a barn fire in the first two months. All took place during spells of cold weather. A heat lamp caused the barn fire, which killed 47 sheep, a steer, four sows, and 35 pigs. The obvious lesson: Don't ever let animals operate heat lamps.

On January 24 an electrical wiring problem caused a smoke scare at the courthouse, but no damage. (As any building ages such problems become more common, and the size of the courthouse alone is enough to make firefighters nervous.) A run to the Noble County Jail in December turned out to be a false alarm, caused when someone noticed steam escape from a roof vent and thought it was smoke. That's the "old" county jail.

(As mentioned earlier, the Old Jail is now a museum just west of the courthouse, and a garage on that property contains the AFD's second hose cart and one of Avilla's.)

As spring neared, more grass fire reports came in along the railroad tracks, including two on the same day, within half a mile of each other. In a ten year period eleven similar fires sprouted up; some stretched for miles along the tracks and into neighboring fields.

Some were caused accidentally, by sparks; others, not so accidentally. No cooperation came from railroad companies, and firefighters began to think of railroad executives as the enemy.

On September 14, a salesman drove up to the Ford Garage at Orange and Hazel streets, and walked inside. When he saw his car again it was on fire, but luckily the firehouse stood half a block away. If the fire happened five years later, it would have been in front of the fire station itself, converted from the auto dealership.

Not so Mobile

The last month Harry Metz served as fire chief – March, 1959 – was a busy one, starting with Albion's first recorded mobile home fire on the first day of the month. Because of their light construction, mobile homes burn quickly and at high temperatures, and are often gutted before fire units can arrive. Although this one was in town limits (on Oak Street), it burned down.

For a long time mobile homes that caught fire outside town limits were, like barn fires, doomed by long response times, construction, and lack of water. Firefighters accepted that they could only protect exposures.

But new construction techniques make mobile homes somewhat less volatile, and firefighters constantly adapt new techniques and equipment to do their jobs better. Now firefighters aggressively attack such fires if there's any hope at all

to at least save some of the contents, if not the structure itself. This brings up a whole new discussion about how much firefighters should be willing to endanger their own safety to

Albion firefighters change breathing air tanks and prepare to finish extinguishing a mobile home fire on the south side of town. Generators on the ground power fans to force smoke from the building

protect property.

Meanwhile, "controlled" burns spread to cause a minor roof fire and four grass fires in March. But on March 17 a fire of more mysterious origin broke out in Brimfield.

Fire in Your Drawers

Fire trucks from Albion and Kendallville answered the alarm at 10:30 p.m., and arrived as smoke filled the second floor of a home near the center of Brimfield – if Brimfield can be called large enough to have a center. Twelve Albion firefighters coupled hose from the tanker to the '52, set up flood lights from the utility truck, and searched for the blaze.

Many fires start or spread into hidden spaces, such as between walls, but this hidden space proved a bit more unusual. A firefighter opened the drawer of a bedroom chest and had to jump back when flames shot out at him. The blaze was quickly controlled after causing an estimated $300 damage, but how it started in a closed drawer remained a mystery; perhaps someone had money burning a hole in their pocket.

After serving as chief for five years, Harry Metz turned the position over to Robert Beckley in 1959. Beckley's first year as chief stayed busy, with small but potentially major fires at the Brimfield Truck Stop and Frick's Saw Mill, calls for the water truck at two barn fires near Avilla, and a barn fire at the "Old Sam Baker farm" in the new Chain O' Lakes State Park. (There's a state park in Missouri named after Sam A. Baker – presumably not the same man.)

The volunteers found time during all this to sign up for a first aid class. They hadn't been involved in a lot of medical training or responses in the past, but that would change in a big way.

By far the most serious incident the AFD was involved in that year took place on the other side of Kendallville.

HazMat? What's That?

Rain fell at 8 p.m. on October 24, when a semi-truck traveling over US 6 skidded on a slippery pavement, overturned, and rolled down a steep embankment near the Morr Bros. Foundry. The driver escaped with an arm injury, and it seemed at first the incident would be minor.

The semi's fuel tanks began to leak, but the steady rain lessened any danger of an ignition. (Back then few fussed over cleaning up fuel spills.) The truck had no markings to indicate a hazardous load, but to be on the safe side emergency workers called the shipper at Niagara Falls, NY.

That's when they discovered the truck carried the flammable and toxic trichlorene ethylene, a not-so-fun chemical. But wait – there's more. The load also contained 54 barrels of sodium peroxide, each weighing 480 pounds. The latter substance could react violently with oil – such as from ruptured fuel tanks – or water – such as from the still falling rain.

Oops.

The shipper also warned if the sodium peroxide caught fire it would produce a toxic gas, and could explode when sprayed with water. The Indiana State Police set up blockades to keep traffic away, and the Kendallville Fire Department stretched hoselines, unsure if they could do anything except evacuate if a fire started.

(There's a common expression in the fire service, which relates to picking the right ladder length for a job: "You can stretch a hoseline, but you can't stretch a ladder". Why is laying out an attack hoseline called **stretching** the hose? Fire hose actually does lengthen a bit when it's charged with water under pressure, but not enough to explain where the term came from.)

Because of the distance from the nearest fire hydrant, Albion's tanker got the call at 9 p.m. to provide extra water. Around midnight another truck arrived to transfer the cargo to safety, along with a wrecker to turn the damaged semi upright; it took almost 12 hours more to complete the operation. In the meantime several damaged drums, leaking peroxide, turned up. Three explosions led to small fires, but the firefighters managed to quench them without causing more serious problems.

As if things weren't bad enough, the Albion tanker got involved in another incident that night, involving the world's oldest hazardous material – alcohol. As John Beckley drove the truck, shuttling water to the scene, a car t-boned it at the intersection of Kendallville's Main and Rush streets.

No one was hurt, and the driver of the car went to jail for driving under the influence and failure to yield the right of way to an emergency vehicle. And the tanker? Well, back in those days trucks were more solidly built: It sustained $10 worth of damage – that's not a typo – and continued with the water shuttle operation.

As the years passed after the semi crash, laws that dealt with hazardous materials became stricter, and such materials are now supposed to be clearly marked. But these materials – liquids, gases and solids – are transported in greater quantities than ever, and firefighters know from sad experience that HazMat incidents can happen any time, any place.

CHAPTER TEN

New Station – New Service
Or,
Load Up the U-Haul, We're Moving Next Door

The Sixties

According to an old 7 Up commercial, the sixties were a time of agonizing reappraisal. Well, reappraisal, anyway. Although hazardous materials had to be addressed, more "routine" matters needed attention, especially for a small fire department with a limited budget.

For instance, in August, 1960, the firefighters pressure tested the department's fire hose, and 400 feet of it failed. Fire hose must be tested every year – yet another chore for the volunteers – and when it ruptures under 250 psi of pressure, it fails spectacularly and dangerously.

In September of the same year, "bad holes" opened in the water tank of the '52, now only eight years old. We're talking about a truck made of metal that circulates water as its main job, so rust is no surprise in the days before undercoating. In October, the battery on the '29 had to be replaced.

Of course, fires continued, and each fire cost the AFD in gasoline, maintenance, and compensation (now up to $2 an hour) for the volunteers. By the end of the 20th century, after figuring in costs such as insurance and utilities, fire officials estimate it costs $2,000 just to roll the trucks out the doors to a call. The bigger the fire, the more the extra cost, and five house fires came in during 1960.

Routine operating costs ate up the AFD budget, so few special preparations were made for uncommon hazards such as spilled chemicals. Mitigating spills, then as now, could cost a pretty penny – a pretty corroded, poisoned, contaminated penny.

The volunteers also began to wish for a four wheel drive truck for field fires, but it would have to wait another five years. With wildland fires, as with structure fires, firefighters became impatient to take the fight to the seat of the blaze, rather than attacking defensively.

There was also the cost of a muck fire in 1960. Muck fires burn underground in organic material that looks like soil but is flammable when dry, and can be almost impossible to put out. For an entire day in October, Robert Beckley and Jack Robinson shuttled 17,000 gallons of water to a site out of town, in an attempt to smother a smoldering blaze.

"Big Barn Fire"... are there small ones?

Two particularly bad barn fires broke out in 1960. The first burned a huge structure on the Paul Norden farm, southwest of Lisbon in eastern Noble County, and caused $30,000 damage.

Albion, Kendallville, and Avilla fire units converged on the blaze to no avail, and fell back to a defensive operation to protect exposures. Destroyed inside the barn were a truck, three tractors, a combine, manure spreader, corn picker, "a large quantity of hay", some grain, and an adjoining milk house. Three calves were also killed. One can only imagine the size of this barn, even by barn standards.

The second fire was closer to home, three miles from Albion on County Road 500N. Albion fire trucks

Barn fires burn so hot that water streams often have to be turned onto adjoining buildings to keep them from bursting into flames. As with fires in Albion's early history, it can be impossible to save the building of fire origin.

arrived at the Ira Wright farm to find another large barn engulfed in flames. Around it stood over a dozen other buildings, all of them endangered. To make matters worse, another structure connected to the burning one: a 76x70 foot building with sheet metal sides and roof.

A metal shell helps protect exposures from radiant heat. It also makes getting a water stream on the fire more difficult, especially when the roof collapses on large amounts of burning interior.

Although the barn was lost, firefighters were determined to save what they could. With the assistance of Kendallville, Ligonier, and Noble Township units, they fought the blaze for more than four hours as it consumed a mower, spreader, and 7,000 bales of hay. They pumped water from a large ditch in addition to using a tanker shuttle, and managed to save the attached structure as well as other endangered buildings.

A Call For Help

But the biggest fire of 1960, reminiscent of those that once erupted regularly in Albion's business district, waited until December 23.

At 12:30 a.m. the blaze erupted at the Farm Store in Ligonier, and before the night ended it gutted a barber shop and insurance agency, then jumped into the Eagles Lodge in an adjoining building. The Ligonier Fire Department's call for help was answered by engines from Albion, Cromwell and Syracuse (more departments likely responded, but weren't listed in local news accounts). The combined force didn't complete the job until about 8 a.m., and by then $120,000 damage had been done.

Those who complain about emergency response times should know what happened when the '52 responded to this fire. First of all, eight volunteers went with it. I'd imagine they took another, unreported truck with them, or some of the volunteers drove their personal vehicles, because the '52 could hold three men in its cab – small men. Most likely the utility truck went along.

But whether the other men followed or rode on the tailboard – a hazardous but common practice even on fires out of town – they found their response delayed. As they made their way west on US 6, the firefighters got behind a "big truck", as the *Albion New Era* put it. Nothing – siren, flashing lights, yells or waving hands – could convince the driver to pull over and let them by.

It wasn't the last time this would happen. The fact is, a delayed fire response (when it isn't in the imagination of excited bystanders at the scene) usually isn't the firefighters' fault.

1961:Conflagration

Two particularly bad fires happened in 1961, and the second hit very close to home.

The Industrial Engineering Company in Brimfield, said the *Albion New Era*, manufactured "specialty farm equipment, industrial mowers, and special material handling equipment for industry". On a Saturday afternoon in October, five employees worked inside the one story cement block and wood structure.

At 1:20 p.m. the workers discovered flames in the eastern part of the factory, and turned in an alarm. Albion, Kendallville, and Rome City firefighters responded, but a stiff breeze pushed flames through the building, and soon through the roof. Help came from Ligonier and Wolcottville, but their tankers emptied quickly, and while the water trucks went for another load the engines had only the limited water in their onboard tanks to use.

Still, the firefighters confined the blaze to about two-thirds of the building, helped by a fire wall dividing that portion from the rest. But $60,000 damage resulted, with most of the roof burned and collapsed.

It's interesting to note the way the *Kendallville News-Sun* identified the responding fire departments: "Kendallville, Rome City, Ligonier, Jefferson Township, Johnson Township, Green Township and York Township responded."

In Indiana, the law makes townships responsible for fire protection. Sometimes township trustees contract for fire protection with town or city officials within the township, or with neighboring communities. Sometimes the volunteers start their own department, funded by the township or by efforts of firefighters themselves. That's why, for instance, the fire department based in Wolcottville is called the Johnson Township Fire Department.

When the paper referred to the Jefferson, Green, and York Townships, they meant the Albion Fire Department, which provides protection to those and to Albion Township. The town provided the fire station, while the townships jointly owned the '39 and '52 pumpers and contributed a share of the annual budget. So, the AFD could technically be called the "Town of Albion and Townships of Albion, York, Jefferson, and Green Fire Department", or the AAYFGFD.

You can imagine what a nightmare lettering the side of the truck could be. And helmets? Each helmet would have to hold a billboard. But all those townships did get listed on some of the trucks, right up into the 70s. For the sake of convenience, the department continued to be called the AFD.

On a Saturday afternoon a week after the Brimfield fire, a blaze broke out across the street from the Albion fire station, in the Smith Brothers' Plumbing and

Heating Shop south of the Courthouse square. Sixteen of Albion's eighteen volunteers were available to respond the '52 and '39.

But the fire jumped ahead of them to engulf the structure near the center of the block, then spread to an adjoining barn. Soon three engines and thirty firefighters from the Rome City and Wolf Lake fire departments hurried on the way.

The '29, now over thirty years old, seldom saw use. Few fires broke out that two engines couldn't handle, and the '29 worked more as a parade truck than an in-service apparatus. But it stayed equipped and in working order just in case, and that precaution paid off. After all, while most fires required two engines, the operative word is *most*.

Desperate to control the flames, which now spread to a storage building owned by Riddle and Metz Hardware, the AFD put their '29 into action, as reported by the *Kendallville News-Sun*:

"Albion's 1929 pumper – a mighty mite that pumped 500 gallons on the flames, keeping up with the best of them." The writer meant 500 gallons *per minute*, since a total of 500 gallons didn't mean much on this conflagration. However, the '29 actually has a 300 gpm pump.

A car parked between the barn and the plumbing and heating shop caught fire, and the heat was too intense for anyone to get near it. The vehicle belonged to Byron Smith, who operated the burning store – and inside the car laid a butane gas container. (This was likely the same Byron Smith who headed the AFD from 1952-54.)

Albion Firefighters reposition the hoseline during a windblown fire involving a mobile home with a structure built around it.

Downtown fires, as with this one years later but on the same block of South Orange Street as the 1961 blaze, can go from bad to worse very fast.

Caught between two structure fires, the car caught fire itself from the radiant heat, and then the butane tank exploded. The blast knocked down and stunned Albion firemen Jay Davis and Jim Jackson, but they weren't seriously injured.

Mutual aid companies arrived to put more water on the blaze, and as the sun went down the AFD utility truck came in to help light the fire scene. After three hours, firefighters pushed the flames back and brought the fire under control.

In addition to the three most involved structures, several others were damaged: The Land Bank office, a tavern, a dry-cleaning shop and clothing store, and the Albion Hotel on the courthouse square, where the fire burned through a back door before firefighters stopped it.

The spot where the fire started is now a parking lot between the Eagles Lodge and the courthouse square. On the other side of York Street, a barn damaged by the blaze burned down itself, three years later. That property is now an empty lot, owned by the town of Albion.

1962 was a banner year: During a July heat wave which produced still-standing temperature records, a baby boy was born in Kendallville; he would someday grow up to write the history of the Albion Fire Department.

But enough about me.

Weather really was a big factor of 1962, and it denied the firefighters a chance to rest. A cold snap hit in early January, with the temperature reaching four below zero, and four structure fires broke out in two days. It must have stayed cold in March – an electric blanket caught fire early that month. Possibly the blanket did its job a bit too well.

Dry replaced cold, and on April 21 three woodland fires came in, two of them inside the area of Chain O' Lakes State Park. They burned, according to one report, "grass and old buildings". Over the next several years a rash of fires struck the park, leveling barns, old abandoned homes, a cottage, and an old log cabin, as well as large areas of brush and grass. Because the underbrush in the park had few natural firebreaks and grew without control, ground cover fires there tended to be severe, and Albion firefighters fought dozens of them over a ten year period.

Once again the largest fire of the year waited until December, when the Marchland Truck Stop west of Brimfield burned down. $40,000 damage resulted as the blaze ripped through a two story concrete block and metal building, which housed a garage and restaurant.

Despite the efforts of Albion, Rome City and Kendallville firefighters, the blaze then jumped to a one story office building and gutted it, before being doused after several hours.

Ambulance

After four years as chief, Robert Beckley turned the position over to Assistant Chief Al Jacob in 1963. Both men knew the AFD faced major changes.

For several years the AFD, equipped with a resuscitator and basic first aid training, stood ready to help, but local funeral homes provided ambulance service to area towns. That would soon change.

Why did funeral homes provide ambulance service? After all, didn't saving people go against their basic business model? Well (you may not want to dwell on this too much), patients could be laid down in the hearses. In cots, I mean, not coffins – let's not get scary.

Although the funeral homes had the vehicles, there was little training, and no standardization of equipment. They scooped up the patient and drove like hell to the hospital, hoping he'd survive the trip. (You have to wonder how much stress the patients underwent when they looked up to see a hearse pull to a stop beside them.)

The funeral homes did the best they could, but by the early sixties new rules and regulations, along with insurance demands, killed their ambulance business.

Now, with no one else to do it, the volunteers took up the challenge and readied themselves with rescue and first aid training. In the April 4, 1963 issue of the *American* this short item appeared: "Albion, Jefferson, Green, and York Townships have jointly purchased a Rescue Unit vehicle, to be housed in the Albion Utility building, ready for any emergency needs of this community, according to Fire Chief Al Jacob. It is completely equipped with siren, red flasher light, stretcher-cot, oxygen and resuscitator. Members of the fire department who have received special training will answer the Rescue Unit calls."

The truck also held basic first aid equipment. In fact, the AFD's first responders have more equipment on hand these days, even though they don't transport patients anymore. Modern ambulances carry way more gear, of course.

The AFD ambulance works an accident on the Courthouse Square, back in the 60s.(Photo courtesy Phil Jacob)

A 1951 Buick, painted light blue and white, became the AFD medics' first ambulance. Later they purchased a 1958 Cadillac, then a white 1966 Oldsmobile. For over a decade the AFD provided ambulance service to the area, until the Noble County EMS was created in 1974.

Gently Used Fire Station

The arrival of an ambulance helped force another change on the AFD: Once again, their firehouse seemed to shrink. It was first built in 1930 to hold a pumper, chemical engine and two hose carts. Thirty years later three engines, a tanker, utility pickup, and ambulance were crammed into the upstairs and basement truck bays.

Where could the new station be located? Right next door, to the south, stood a readymade replacement. Once a Ford auto dealership, the two story structure already had more than enough garage area for all the trucks, plus rooms for meetings and training. There was no need to look further.

At first one overhead door led from the new apparatus bay, and the trucks lined up diagonally so they could all get out (hopefully no two drivers would try to leave at the same time). When the '29 retired for good, it spent some time in the old auto showroom on the southwest corner, which for years still sported the large display windows. Later the town added two more overhead doors, and blocked in the showroom when the police department moved into part of the building.

This photo, from the late 50s or early 60s, shows the Albion Town Hall/Firehouse on the left. On the right is the auto dealership that became the fire station in the 60s. Between is a storefront, later town down, built on the site of the town's second firehouse.

The old fire station was converted to a garage for the street department, and served in that capacity for twenty years. For several years after it again housed an emergency vehicle, until Noble County EMS #6 moved from the (again) overcrowded fire station to the old firehouse in the 80s.

At about the same time the fire department moved, four of its members – Howard Campbell, Keith Seymore, Dale Guthrie, and former chief Robert Beckley – retired. The volunteers toasted their retiring members on February 11, 1963 with a steak supper.

CHAPTER ELEVEN

Disasters and Near Disaster
Or
Yes, it can get worse

Another event of 1963 was anything but pleasant, and something all firefighters dread: a fire death.

While Betty Clouse slept on April 7, 1963, fire broke out in the garage attached to her High Street home. Her husband got their children out as flames spread into the two story residence, but he couldn't battle his way back through the heat and smoke.

Fourteen firefighters contained the flames to the kitchen and bedroom, but couldn't save Mrs. Clouse. Dr. Sneary, county coroner at the time, declared the cause of death suffocation. Albion firefighters would be faced by a similar tragedy less than ten years later.

Farm Conflagration

On October 26, 1963, a "routine" barn fire broke out on the Wayne Applegate farm, southwest of Albion. We know by now "routine" fires seldom are, don't we? Once again, wind and a lack of water combined to increase the threat.

The blaze started in the west loft, and a stiff breeze fanned it to engulf the structure. Soon a brooder house and machinery building caught fire, and Albion firefighters arrived to find radiant heat battering the south side of the farm's home.

They called Wolf Lake and Cromwell for help, then Kendallville for another tanker, but by the time help arrived the house was on fire.

With the outbuildings lost, firemen concentrated on dousing the house fire, then had to keep it cooled until the barn fire died down. They had to brave severe radiant heat to get close enough to spray water on the home.

They saved the house, but two firefighters, Jack Robinson and Carl Gaff, suffered burns on their faces, arms and necks. They were treated at the Albion Clinic while their colleagues finished extinguishing the flames.

This is a dangerous business, and it doesn't matter whether you're a volunteer or career firefighter. Safety equipment and training may lessen the risk, but can't eliminate it. All fires – even the "routine" ones – must be taken seriously.

Minor Improvements

Small fires at John & Mid's Restaurant and Leatherman Bros. served as reminders that destructive business fires like the one in 1961 remained a real possibility, and work continued to update the fire department.

For instance, a two way radio was mounted in the tanker in September, 1964. The $250 Motorola radio would allow the water truck to communicate with the fire station, and with units at the scene, as it shuttled water from the nearest source.

A big innovation in rural water supply came in the form of a 500 gallon folding **dump tank** for the tanker. The canvas tank, supported by a metal frame, would be set up beside an engine, which drafted water from it. The tanker could dump its load into the dump tank (thus the term), then head back for more. This left 1,000 gallons in the dump tank and the engine's booster tank – not a lot, but better than nothing. This shuttle system works so well that most tankers now carry dump tanks.

(A quick reminder on terminology: In the western U.S., tankers are called "tenders". Ask for a tanker in California, and you'll soon see a water laden airplane circling overhead.)

Four Wheel Drive

No matter what else happens, there are always grass fires. Sometimes more, sometimes less, depending on the weather, but since the AFD covers 96 mostly rural square miles the danger is always there. The typical grass fire "season" in Indiana lasts from late March through April, but they can and do happen at any time

86

of the year. In 2010, dry weather resulted in a busy grass fire season in September and October.

The '39's front mounted pump was designed to protect against such fires, because the truck could pump while rolling to work its way around a grass fire front. But on April 13, 1960, the truck got stuck in mud at a grass fire, and the flames then had to be put out by hand. Well, with tools – not literally by hand. Probably.

Area firefighters carry flat rubber mats at the end of wooden handles, usually called **beaters**, as well as fire brooms, shovels, hand held extinguishers, and other hand tools for such work. These fires often take them to places no truck can reach, such as swamps or dense woods.

One way to know you're having a bad day is when your town's water tower runs low, and a tanker shuttle has to be set up right in the middle of the downtown area. Since this fire, a new water tower and improved distribution system has made more water available in Albion.

But if a fire could be reached by four wheel drive vehicle, wouldn't it be a lot easier than hiking in on foot to attack with hand tools?

Because they're weather related, grass fires tend to come in bunches. On October 23, 1963, three happened within a few hours, all on B&O Railroad property within 2 ½ miles of each other. All spread to nearby fields, owned by local farmers Dick Cole, Carl Huff, and George Leatherman.

In April, 1964, six were called in over a three day period. A few days later, another one spread from a trash fire in the dump at Chain O' Lakes State Park. (No longer used for trash, it's near the center of the park not far from Sand Lake.) The

There are many causes of grass fires. Barn fires, for instance.

park, with its large areas of wildland and few roads to serve as a fire break, became a major worry.

In more recent years Department of Natural Resources employees and Department of Corrections inmates built fire roads and widened trails throughout the park, so access and fire spread aren't the danger they once were. However, now that former fields have started to become overgrown, the fire load is much higher.

Winter storms also made the acquisition of a four wheel drive truck, which could serve double duty in deep snow or rough ground, look more attractive.

Albion's first grass unit, often called a grass buggy, arrived in 1965. (Why "buggy"? It looked a little like an overgrown dune buggy.) The 1953 military surplus Dodge truck carried a small water tank, pump, and a reel of hose, as well as hand tools. Like the '39, it could pump and roll, but its lighter weight and design made it less likely to get stuck on soft or uneven ground.

Today no rural fire department would want to do without a four wheel drive, and many – such as the AFD – run more than one.

1965 started with a barn fire, then a mobile home fire in which a nearby barrel of gasoline "caused quite a threat". Gasoline caused a much larger threat on March 21, when a car ran into a gas pump at the DX Station, at Orange and South Streets. The pump caught fire, but firefighters managed to subdue the blaze.

The '29 was now over 35 years old, and the '39, which kept busy on grass fires even after the grass truck went into service, began to show its years. Because of its age, the '29 saw use only in the most extreme emergencies, leaving Albion with two "regular" engines. From past experience, it was obvious the town needed three.

Albion's newest two engines were designed as rural apparatus, so planners decided a "city" truck should come next. Bids advertised by board members Frank W. Foote, Don Davis, and Frank Clouse called for a 750 gpm pump, 25% more powerful than the '52's pump, and more than twice the size of the '39's. Because the townships would help pay for the apparatus, a 500 gallon booster tank (the largest in common use at the time) was added.

The old superstition held true: The big fire came before the truck's delivery, and a slump in calls commenced after it went into service.

The '29 Swan Song?

On October 2, 1965, four months after work began on a new truck, fire ripped through a three family apartment house two blocks south of the fire station. This would be one of the last runs for the '29.

According to Assistant Chief Jim Applegate, the fire started in the basement of the wood frame home and smoldered for some time before it spread upstairs. No one was home; owner Henry Jacob was on a fishing trip to Canada, while his wife visited relatives in LaGrange. The Gustin family, which occupied the rear of the house, was at a movie in Fort Wayne, and they arrived back in Albion around midnight to find themselves homeless.

Byron Powell, a neighbor, spotted the blaze at around 9:15 p.m. and turned in the alarm from the same home where this writer now lives.

Basement fires are notoriously difficult to fight. Ventilation is next to impossible, and firefighters must fight their way through waves of contaminated, superheated air to reach the fire. The volunteers used all three engines and fought for over three hours, but couldn't keep the blaze from gutting the area above the basement, occupied by the Jacobs, and an unrented apartment upstairs.

They did manage to save some belongings of the Gustin family, whose apartment was not over the basement.

After the fire, the men loaded hose back onto the '29, and returned it to the station. Although to this day the truck is in working order, it would see active service only a few more times.

Thanks For the Compliment

No doubt the destruction of the home frustrated the men, despite knowing they did their best. Maybe, then, an article in the November 18, 1965 *Albion New Era* cheered them up, as it recounted a "save":

"Mr. and Mrs. J.C. Roscoe, 208 E. Main Street, Albion, wish to thank all the Albion firemen for the wonderful job they did Sunday in putting out the fire in their home.

"The fire broke out while Mrs. Roscoe was at church Sunday morning, and was contained in the upper floor of the home. Mrs. Roscoe stated they would probably have lost their entire home had another five minutes elapsed before the firemen arrived. As it was because of their quick action only the top floor of the house was burned. There was some water damage to the lower floor around where the fire had burned through the floor, and ceiling and smoke damage was evident throughout the house. Mr. Roscoe, who was home at the time of the fire was uninjured.

"Mrs. Roscoe said they can't thank the firemen enough for the work of putting out the fire and for remaining afterwards to help straighten things up."

For as long as there've been fire departments, there've been many more complaint-happy armchair fire chiefs than people who take the time to thank firefighters for their efforts. (I'm talking more about bystanders; you can't blame a fire victim for being grumpy at the time.) When a volunteer does his best and receives public thanks for it, you can bet he takes notice.

More Truck – Less Runs

Like the '52, the 1965 engine had an American LaFrance pump, this time on a Chevy chassis. The large booster tank and more powerful pump made it perfect for the growing needs of the AFD. Extra compartment space contained, among other auxiliary equipment, two new air packs, which gave firefighters a better chance to reach and extinguish interior fires.

1966, the year after the AFD updated its inventory with two new trucks, was the quietest year for fire calls since 1960. Maybe it really would be good insurance to buy a new truck every year, to cut down on emergencies. Still, AFD members fought a dozen grass fires that year, and the new grass truck performed well.

On February 9, 1967, the new engine got its chance to perform at a house fire caused by a faulty chimney, at 715 E. Hazel Street. The fire burned up a wall and into the attic, but was doused before it got a chance to drop down and gut the rest of the house.

Since both the '52 and the '65 had the same size water tanks, the '52 rolled

first to rural fires, while the '65 was reserved for in town fires where the 750 gpm pump could make use of a steady water supply. The '39 served as a backup truck at first, but over the next several years it saw less and less use, and instead the two newer engines handled most structure fires together.

The '65 fire engine, colored burgundy but never blushing, struts its stuff at the Chain O' Lakes Festival parade.

Disasters, Manmade and Natural

At 4:45 on a Saturday, May 14, 1966, an 80 car freight train hit a broken rail. The resulted was a spectacular pileup of 21 cars, on the east edge of Albion. The AFD responded, along with local and state police units and the Civil Defense (now called the Department of Homeland Security), and all were relieved to find no injuries and no fire.

Several containers of alcohol in one car broke, though, which threatened fire from an explosive liquid that ignites far more readily than gasoline. (Imagine what that does to your stomach?) Emergency units stood by, and cordoned off the area while railroad crews from Garrett and Willard, Ohio began to clear the wreckage

By Sunday morning, trains passed through again. The AFD's role in this operation turned out to be precautionary, although of course it could have been far worse.

The same held true when tornadoes touched down in the area half a dozen times in 1967. The AFD's fire siren doubled as a tornado siren, and its high pitched shriek got a workout that year. No fires, entrapments, or serious injuries resulted from those storms in the Albion area, but as always AFD members stood by to give aid.

Scare on the Square

Sixteen men and a full complement of equipment turned out on July 10, 1967, when a fire was reported at the Noble County Courthouse. But, according to the AFD run report, "The janitor caught some wastepaper on fire, (but) had it out when the trucks arrived".

Even the most gung-ho rookie must have breathed a sigh of relief. A fire in Albion's ornate, tall (by Albion standards) and by-gosh huge courthouse is a firefighter's nightmare.

Another scare on the courthouse square happened on March 15, 1968, when an overheated motor started smoking at the Excel Distribution Corp, on the north side of Jefferson Street. Still another came on September 21, when sulphur candles in the basement of Jim's Hardware caused a false alarm. Knowing how fast a fire in the closely packed courthouse square can get out of control, the volunteers always send a full response to such calls – just in case.

Major fires in Albion held off for several years, but the first month of 1969 saw a hazardous material incident that could have wiped out a good portion of the town.

Passing Gas

At about 11:30 a.m., a Noble County Co-Op truck backed up to a company dock on the south edge of town. The truck's wheels skidded on ice, and the vehicle slid sideways on the sloped drive, then struck a pole that held a transformer and switch box. A piece of angle iron securing the electrical equipment punched a three inch diameter hole into the truck's side.

2,780 gallons of gasoline flooded over the area.

This time the AFD's job became not to fight a fire, but to prevent one. Police Chief Gene Lock, Civil Defense workers, and firefighters blocked off the entire section of town, evacuated several families on Hickory Street, and closed down SR 9 from Walnut to Harrison streets. Several business also had to close.

The gasoline stood ankle deep in some spots (I'd hate to be the ankle that measured it), ready to be ignited by the slightest spark. Two eastbound trains shut down their engines and coasted through the area – a questionable decision, considering the injured tanker truck stood so close to the railroad tracks. It would have been better to stop the trains completely, despite the scheduling nightmare that would result.

Despite the cold weather, home furnaces had to be shut off, as did pilot lights.

The volunteers used a special detergent to break down the gas into less volatile substances, which they washed into the sewers. Not allowed these days! It took almost six hours to finish the cleanup, but emergency workers accomplished their goal and prevented any fire.

About fifty workers from police, fire, and Civil Defense agencies worked together to avert a disaster, while the Red Cross served coffee and sandwiches to people who had just begun to think about lunch when the accident happened. If you don't think the coffee and sandwiches were important, try spending a day like that without them.

This showed the emergency services at their best, working together to avert a catastrophe. If the gasoline ignited, a dozen buildings would be in flames within seconds, and more soon afterward. Many of those who worked to prevent it were in constant danger of being caught in an explosion, and their courage should be noted.

A Busy Time, 1969

The gas spill had the potential to be the worst disaster of the year, but in another sense, all of 1969 became one long disaster. It was the busiest year in the AFD's history up to that point, with a record 66 fire calls and 47 ambulance runs. The volunteers made a total of over 100 responses for the first time ever.

A full 25% of the fire calls were grass fires – 20 in March alone. That same month, a barn and storage sheds owned by Vance Keister, Charlie Campbell, and Assistant Chief Jim Applegate all caught fire from burning grass. Most of those calls came in the middle of an usually dry month: four on March 15, three the next day, four more two days later, and five on March 22.

After 26 fire runs in March, none came in at all in May (with the exception of seven ambulance calls). Rain played a part, thus my new lyrics to an old song:

A May of rain
Will cut down on our pain.

And now you know why I write books, instead of poetry.

Also in 1969 came a little flurry of terrorism: Someone called in two bomb threats against the Central Noble School system, and the AFD went on standby for a bomb scare at neighboring East Noble. An investigation turned up no bombs.

In June a motorcycle burned two blocks west of the fire station, which I mention because motorcycle fires are rare. The first fire response I ever witnessed, as a teenager, involved an Albion crew on a lime-green engine who sprayed down a smoldering motorcycle on North Elm Street. It caused quite a commotion – yes, our neighborhood was *that* boring.

Still, it showed that the advent of gasoline powered transportation kept firefighters busier than they had ever been before. In September, 1969, tractors caught fire inside the Farm Welding & Tractor Repair Shop, run by Dallas King and Everett Tarleton. October brought a scare at the Sun Oil Co., on South York Street, as recorded on a fire department run report: "Trash fire caught a stack of used tires on fire. The tires in turn caught the contents of the building on fire, damaging seven cases of oil."

Four houses, three barns, four sheds, and a garage burned in 1969, as well as five vehicles. Calls dropped to a more "normal" level in the next few years, but the number of runs rose steadily since then, until by the late 80s the average was higher than 1969's level.

A truly brilliant photographer captures the roof falling during a training fire. Or, I just got lucky. Either way, you don't want to be under that.

CHAPTER TWELVE

Controversy and EMS
Or,
If Johnny and Roy can do it ...

The Albion Fire Department in 1970

Jim Applegate served one year as chief in 1970 (although the firefighters would reelect him five years later, and he would be chief at the turn of the next decade). Eighteen volunteers were led by a chief, assistant chief, and captain. Their compensation became $2.50 an hour for fire calls, plus a $50 clothing and car allowance each year.

The clothing and car allowance came in handy, not only because volunteer firefighters needed reliable transportation but because protective firefighting gear still wasn't worn regularly. Department issued clothing consisted of a helmet, rubber coat, boots that could be pulled up to hip length, and gloves. Even when the gear was worn, it wasn't uncommon for collars or pants to be damaged by sparks, or stained by thick smoke. Even these days the smoke smell seeps through full protective clothing: Spend an hour in the acrid product of a grain bin fire and you pretty much have to throw away everything you're got on.

Equipment included four engines, because the members couldn't bear to get rid of the beloved '29, now listed as a "reserve" unit. They also had the '52 tanker, '49 pickup truck, '53 grass truck, and '58 Cadillac ambulance. The trucks carried two portable generators and two portable fire pumps that could be carried close to ponds and ditches.

The average apparatus was 21 years old. To compare, in 1988 the average age was down to 18, and in 2006 it stood at 8. It took a lot of hard work to reduce that figure.

Property in the AFD's 96 square mile response area was then valued at $7,823.965. The AFD operated on a budget of $7,500 in 1969, but by the middle of that busy year expenses had already run over $10,000. Because a fire department's "business" is almost impossible to predict, estimating expenses is just as difficult.

Because of the increased number of calls, maintenance requirements on the higher number of trucks and auxiliary equipment, and the increase in preplanning and knowledge needed to deal with modern fire hazards, by 1969 the AFD already had "in sight a man on duty at all times" as reported by the *Noble County American*. That meant three driver/operators who would work 24 hour on, 48 hour off shifts. Those firefighters would pick up many maintenance, paperwork, and other jobs, as well as getting the first truck out the door faster.

Although a good idea, where would the money come from to pay them? It wasn't until 2005 that a paid firefighter came onboard, and then only one part time position.

This is Only a Drill

On a single day – July 26, 1970, a Sunday – seven disasters occurred around Noble County within a four hour period. Thank goodness it was only a disaster drill put on by the Noble County Civil Defense, to test the readiness of area emergency services. The drills were as follows (follow along, now):

At 9:05 a.m. a Greyhound bus and two cars collided in LaOtto. At 8:35 a nursing home caught fire in Wolf Lake, and workers pressed private vehicles into service to transport victims to area hospitals. At 10:40 a.m. an army plane carrying a nuclear warhead (!) crashed near Hossinger Camp, endangering 150 campers, and a 5 mile wide area including the entire town of Wolcottville had to be evacuated to shelters in Kendallville.

Albion's time came at 10:45, when a wreck was reported on SR 8, east of town. The "injured" included Boy Scouts Kevin Blevins, with a broken neck, and Paul Kitt, with a crushed skull. The AFD ambulance and an engine responded, to treat the injured and guard against fire.

At 11:16 a.m. fire trapped 12 people in a burning recreation center in Ligonier. Moments later someone phoned in a bomb threat at the Ligonier school, and after a 37 minute search a bomb crew located the device. At 12:50 p.m., saboteurs set fire to the Douglas Aircraft plant on CR 800N, and a witness spotted two suspects as they ran from the scene on the Pennsylvania Railroad tracks.

An old barn became the "Douglas Aircraft" plant, donated by the owner and burned in the drill. There were casualties, of course, all treated and transported to the hospital.

When a radiological team reported all clear at the plane crash site, and police captured the saboteurs, the exercise ended.

What a day! It's safe to assume so many different disasters are unlikely to happen at the same time, in the same area. On the other hand, it was a good simulation of how overwhelmed local emergency services might be if a big disaster happened – or a couple of "medium" ones, such as a tornado touchdown damaging a facility with hazardous materials.

A similar drill held on Sunday, May 16, 1971, involved 300 men and women in an exercise that lasted over four hours and involved seven incidents across the county.

In that case, Albion rescue workers responded to an explosion at the Formed Tubes plant in the Albion Industrial Park, which involved the possibility of radioactive materials. Albion Boy Scouts from Troop 507 again played the victims – three injuries and one fatality. The fire department ambulance helped treat and transport patients, while other firefighters and Civil Defense workers monitored the area for radioactivity.

To this day the AFD has in its stores a Geiger counter from the era – just in case – which we all hope will never be needed.

More recent disaster drills usually involve one incident, but require mutual aid from across the county. Such complicated, large scale exercises take the cooperation and preplanning of numerous agencies: fire departments, local and state police, hospitals, Civil Defense (now called Emergency Management), Red Cross, and the media.

After 9/11, Civil Defense agencies across the country became Homeland Security or Emergency Management departments, and the dangers they're designed to guard against changed in priority from large scale nuclear attack to natural disasters, hazardous material releases, and terrorist threats.

Many small town residents are convinced they face little danger from terrorist attacks, but they might be fooling themselves: Large scale attacks from well-known groups are not the only threat. Besides, many of the ways to prepare for an act of war are the same things people should do to prepare for natural disasters – and only the foolish believe they don't face that possibility.

Another Tragedy

In 1971 Edward Moorhouse, former secretary and assistant chief for the AFD, took over as chief. Unfortunately, one of the first challenges he faced during his term was another fire death.

Fire ripped through a Green Township house on CR 300E, south of Baseline Road, on April 12, 1972. By the time fire units arrived flames had spread through much of the home, and the volunteers faced a difficult battle.

After they controlled the blaze, firefighters found the body of 89 year old Maude Brumbaugh not far from an outside door, where she had been felled by smoke inhalation before the first fire truck arrived on the scene.

It was far from the last fire death in Noble County.

(The AFD returned to the same farm in October, 1987, when a barn that once stood near the house burned down.)

More Water

More improvements came in the early 70s. The AFD obtained An all-wheel drive army truck from the DNR, used to fight grass fires or battle through snowstorms. Like the Dodge grass buggy, it was equipped with a water tank, pump, and hose.

There was still the problem of getting water to rural fires. The thousand gallons on Albion's tanker didn't go far, when the '65 pumper could drain both the tanker and its own booster tank in two minutes. The firefighters purchased a semi tank truck from a fuel company and equipped it for rural water supply; it held many times the amount of water as the older tanker.

But the semi turned out to be difficult to drive, and handicapped by poor maneuverability on narrow country roads. The tank also tended to leak, and overall the volunteers became dissatisfied with it. The truck stayed in service for a few years before its tank was scrapped, and tractor sold.

Noble County EMS

This notice appeared in December, 1972, Albion papers:

"Due to the difficulty in getting qualified manpower and changes in the State Law requirements pertaining to the ambulance – it will be necessary to suspend and cease ambulance service from the Fire Department as it is now offered. This will take effect January 7, 1973 – Albion Town Board."

New laws required better equipped ambulances and more training for those who manned them. Many of the volunteers couldn't, for various reasons, spend the time and effort required to maintain the new certification requirement: Emergency Medical Technician. Once the new laws went into effect, it would be hard to find enough qualified volunteer firefighters to run the ambulance 24 hours a day.

In addition to the training problems, and the strain on the fire budget to run an ambulance, there was another problem: What if an ambulance run came in while all the AFD members fought a fire? Or vice versa? The problem didn't entirely go away, because several of the volunteers did get the EMT certification to run on the new ambulance system. But non-firefighters also trained to man the new unit, easing the manpower crunch.

The Town Board wouldn't leave its citizens without ambulance service: At the time of the newspaper announcement, a new county-wide EMS system was in the works. Noble County government, fire departments, McCray Hospital (the only hospital in the county at the time, now known as Parkview-Noble), and other involved agencies planned a system to have all ambulances in Noble County directed by one agency. This would standardize training and equipment.

Despite the notice, the AFD continued to run the Albion ambulance until April, 1974. Then the newly organized Noble County EMS took over, and that chapter of the AFD's history ended. For several years EMS #6 was housed at the Albion fire station, before it moved next door – to the *old* Albion fire station.

Rescue Squad

Terry Campbell served as fire chief in 1974, the year the AFD stopped ambulance service and decided to replace the ambulance with a rescue squad.

Each new engine had more available compartment space than the one before it, but still not enough to carry all the new firefighting equipment, such as air packs, portable pumps, and the resuscitator. After all, most of that equipment didn't even exist when the '39 and the '52 went into service, so they hadn't been designed to hold it. A new vehicle was needed to carry the extra gear.

Dedicated rescue units would become more and more popular across the county, but the 1972 Chevy Step Van the AFD purchased in 1974 would be more accurately described as a supply van, or equipment truck. Much of its interior filled up with a rack to hold the volunteers' helmets, boots, and coats in case some of them went straight to the fire, instead of the station.

By the 80s, the firefighters' protective clothing, or **turnout gear**, hung on hooks on the fire station walls after room ran out in the van. Still, the vehicle held little rescue equipment on board, and was better termed a "squad" than a "rescue". Its main use remained fireground support.

The white van carried air packs and extra tanks, power generators, firefighting foam and equipment, flood lights, extension cords, and some hand tools. It could also carry several firefighters, but held only two seats – and riding in the back could be an adventure.

Over the years things would begin to change, as the van filled with more rescue and first aid equipment. Ironically, at about the same time it became more dedicated toward rescue, its designation changed from "Rescue 1" to "Squad 1".

Albion's first rescue truck ...

And second, carrying on a white delivery van theme.

Controversies and Plans

James Applegate, Sr. (as is common in the fire service, Jr. also became a fireman) again took over as fire chief in 1975, just in time for a year filled with controversies.

To a large extent, the argument involved communications. Members of the AFD worked out a plan to move the police department into the station, along with EMS #6 and the fire department. Full time dispatchers would be hired, to take calls for all three services. But the Town Board, already embroiled in an argument over the demotion of Town Marshal Gene Lock, was less than enthusiastic about the idea.

The volunteers, who according to the *News-Sun* cited a continued "lack of response from the board on various matters in the past", sent out a statement along with a public opinion poll. The AFD explained their case by giving the other controversy as an example:

"It seems that the Albion Town Board has complete control of all facets of our local departments. This in itself sounds fine, if they are listening to and trying to do what the people who elected them are asking … but when a large group of taxpayers are interested enough in the Police Department to go to a Town Board Meeting to ask why our Town Marshal has been demoted and get no answer – ARE THEY REALLY LISTENING? The taxpayers were told that the Town Marshal serves at the pleasure of said Town Board.

"On the basis of this statement the Fire Chief, Town Marshal or the head of any department is in that capacity in name only, with no real control over his department. Can a man do a good job when he knows he need only please the Town Board and not the people?

"We need changes and think it not only a legal issue that something be done to update the Fire Department, but it is also a moral obligation."

The authors then made their case for consolidation of the AFD, EMS, and APD into the same place: "We have five EMT's trained but unable to serve the community because, not being firemen, they do not get the calls for an ambulance. Only firemen have telephones for emergency calls." (At the time some EMT's had radio operated pagers, but firefighters had none.) "We do have several firemen but they should not have to handle all calls and are not always available as they do have to work for a living."

A large part of the problem had to do with the AFD's telephone alarm system. For some time, the people of Albion called the same number (2345, as I recall) for both fire and ambulance service. When the Noble County EMS came around, a separate number was established for ambulance calls, but many people continued to call the fire number out of habit and ignorance of the change.

The fire number rang into the homes of the fire department members, and so set off about 19 phones. As of January 31, 1975, as the *News-Sun* article explained: "Some (firemen) hang up after they are sure another fireman has responded to the call. (AFD spokesman Jerry) Morr says this confuses some people who think they have been disconnected."

A side note may explain some of the politics involved: Town Marshal Lock had been a member of the AFD, which might help explain the firefighters' displeasure at his demotion. At least one of the Town Board members at the time had left the fire department, according to some witnesses under less than pleasant circumstances, and some thought he harbored a grudge against the department. Jerry Morr later left the fire department, and himself became a Town Board member.

All I can add to this is, having been an Albion Town Council member myself (name change for the group, there), I suspect the Town Board couldn't legally discuss the demotion because it qualified as a personnel issue. That would cause certain privacy laws to kick in.

Continuing with the article: "One person (responding to the poll) expressed her distress at being answered with a 'meek hello' instead of an assuring voice with an informative 'Albion EMS'." That person continued, "All the while you hear telephone receivers clicking in your ear."

A caller had to dial the new EMS number in order to reach the EMS dispatcher, who worked in Kendallville. The dispatcher could then page out Albion's seven EMTs, but couldn't trigger the fire phones to notify AFD members who also served as EMTs. Conversely, a call to the fire number did not result in the notification of non-firefighter EMTs.

A dispatcher at the Albion fire station, with all three emergency departments under the same roof and tie-ins to both phone systems, could take a call and immediately notify the proper personnel.

Forty of Albion's thousand or so people responded to the poll. Only one respondent lived outside town limits, which indicates the township residents didn't realize how much this problem might affect them. Of those who did respond, 96.29% favored all three agencies in the same building; 85.18% wanted full time dispatchers; 80.37% did not object to a tax increase to fund those changes; 85.18% agreed "The emergency medical service is working successfully in our area"; and the same number had no complaints about the AFD or EMS.

But just 29.62% answered yes to the last question: "Do you feel that the fire department should have definite guidelines for its operation prescribed by the Town Board?" Many of the respondents said they didn't clearly understand the question. Morr explained: "We wanted to know if the people felt the board should set guidelines and let the fire department operate within them under the direction of the fire chief." He said the AFD had asked for specific guidelines, but received no response.

In the *Kendallville News-Sun*, Town Board President John Beckley (also from a long time Albion firefighting family) responded: "We explained our position on different things and thought they understood what the reasons were for not getting things they asked for. If the chief wants guidelines, I imagine they can be written down."

Beckley also said the ambulance service had nothing to do with Albion or the fire department, and should not concern the firefighters. He must have meant financially, because ambulance protection was and is, of course, of critical interest to both the people of Albion and the residents engaged in one of the country's most dangerous professions: firefighting. On a more concrete level, Morr reminded everyone that some firefighters answered the call to service as EMTs, which made it very much their business.

The dispatchers never got hired for the same reason Albion didn't get paid firefighters on duty: money. Eventually the police department did move in and occupy the west part of the first floor, and the three agencies shared the building for several years until first the EMS, then the fire department, moved out. The Albion PD then took over the entire building, which also held a room used – perhaps ironically – for Albion Town Council meetings.

The communication problem eased with the purchase of pagers for firefighters as well as EMTs, and all emergency calls in the Albion area are now routed to dispatchers at the Noble County Sheriff's Department.

In 1976, after a yearlong discussion, $6,531 was allocated for a new radio system in the Albion fire station, which had the capability to page out both the firefighters and EMS #6 members. The base station radio cost $133; the encoder (which "opens" pagers to alert the recipient) cost $338; twenty pagers complete with batteries and charges were $5,960; and installation totaled $100.

So, while the Sheriff's Department dispatch center paged out most fire and EMS calls, the AFD's system remained (and remains) available as a backup. From then on, firefighters never had to worry about missing calls because of being away from the phone, or in an area where they couldn't hear the fire siren.

How Old is Too Old?

In 1975, the AFD began to accept men between the ages of 18 and 21 as "auxiliary firemen". Mindful of recent problems, Chief Jim Applegate asked for and received assurance from the Town Board that this met with their approval. Within five years the rules changed again, so anyone who had reached the age of 18 could come on as a regular member, which allowed me to join on my eighteenth birthday in 1980.

But a few months after the initial decision came another question of age, this one the polar opposite of minimum ages.

During a busy first Town Board meeting of 1976 the Board found time to question Jim Applegate's reappointment as chief. AFD by-laws limited the age for that position to 50, but Applegate was 53. The board accepted Applegate as chief for 30 days, while they researched the matter.

They met again in May, having discovered a town ordinance put forward several years before that said the chief must retire at 50. But they could find no resolution to pass the ordinance in meeting minutes – which meant it wasn't an actual law. They instructed town attorney Paul Barcus to continue checking.

Meanwhile a few former volunteers, some of whom had been forced to retire when they reached the mandatory age, complained about Applegate's continued service. Town Board member Ted Frymier, a former fireman, insisted 53 was "too damn old" to be chief. But Barcus must not have found that resolution; Applegate continued in the post until 1981, then as assistant chief for a few years more. The AFD has since abolished all mandatory retirement ages from their own by-laws.

A New Addition?

In 1975 town leaders discussed plans for a new annex, which would connect the old fire station to the new one. The projected two story building would house public restrooms, communications, storage, and city vehicles – and would be built on land once occupied by Albion's second firehouse.

In October, C.R. Weber and Associates showed the Town Board sketches of the proposed addition, and ideas to remodel the present structures. The new building itself would cost $40,000.

But in March, 1976, the Board received word that their application for funds from the Department of Housing and Urban Development had been turned down. There was some further discussion, but the money never came together for the project.

How much this would have affected the AFD is unknown; the addition would have mostly relieved cramped conditions in the Town Hall. Later suggestions for building or parking areas were never followed up on, and the area, where a small wooden commercial building once stood after the firehouse was moved, remained empty of all except sometimes flooded parking for town vehicles. A later addition to the east side of the fire station limited parking for firefighters, but before that could be addressed the fire department moved again.

Members of the AFD pose for a photo in front of their newest truck, in the late 70s. (Photo courtesy Albion Fire Department)

CHAPTER THIRTEEN

Firehouse Damage and the Lime-Green Lemon
Or,
It seemed like a good idea at the time ...

Let's go back to 1974, before all the controversies broke out, when the Town Board accepted and took under advisement bids for a new fire engine – a truck which in itself would become controversial.

Like the '65, the new engine would be a "city" truck to deal with the increased fire protection problems of modern times, and it seemed the new apparatus would soon be in the department's possession. But as arguments raged on other fronts, problems developed with the truck. It would be another two years before it backed into the firehouse.

(In the same 1974 meeting, by the way, the AFD purchased a portable radio to allow a firefighter inside an incident to communicate with trucks or dispatchers outside. It's seen as dangerous and irresponsible, nearly forty years later, for a crew to work inside a hazard area without a radio.)

In September, 1975, American Fire Apparatus announced the pumper would arrive in February, just over a year after bids were accepted. The next month, at Chief Applegate's request, Town Board President John Beckley checked into the matter, and wasn't encouraged.

February came and went, and no fire truck appeared.

In March, 1976, the town received word the truck would be delivered that summer, "Hopefully in August". John Dickman, a representative of American Fire

Apparatus, appeared at a Board meeting and blamed the delay on a slump in business.

A slump in business indeed; unbeknownst to anyone in Albion, the company was "slumping" toward bankruptcy.

Dickman also claimed Albion was lucky – a nearby fire department ordered a truck from them on March 9, 1974, and didn't get it until a few days before that meeting – two years after they placed an order.

In May, Applegate reported the delivery date had been moved up to July, and also that the company had made a mistake that would work in Albion's favor:

The engine came with a 300 gallon booster tank – but the AFD had asked for a 500 gallon tank, the same size carried on the '65 and the '52. Going bigger cost the town an extra $400, but to make up for it the company threw in an additional compartment between the pump and the cab, at no extra cost.

The larger water tank was one of the selling points when town officials asked the area township trustees, at a special meeting on May 11, to help pay for the engine. Because of the delays, the town scrambled to reinvest money earmarked for the apparatus, from revenue sharing, cumulative fire building, and equipment funds. Much of the money had been placed into 90 day certificates of deposit – much longer than 90 days ago.

At the time, trustees to the townships covered by the AFD included J.C. Boner, William Huff, Robert Moore, and Leland McCoy. After discussing, as the *News-Sun* reported, "the truck and the services the Albion Fire Department provides for the townships", the trustees reacted favorably. They talked over the situation with their advisory boards, then agreed to help, in return for continued full service from the AFD.

But July came and went, and still no truck.

In September Applegate reported to the Town Board a plan to travel to Bristol for preliminary testing of the engine. But he added the vehicle hadn't been painted yet, and he thought the company would "be hurting" to complete it by the new due date, October 1st.

He was right.

Finally!

The new fire engine made its public debut at Central Noble High School's Homecoming parade on October 22, 1976 – one year and nine months after being ordered. The *Noble County American* ran a front page picture of Applegate driving the truck in the parade, captioned: "Here at last".

At an open house on December 3, 1976, the firefighters parked the new truck beside the '29, for comparison. The new fire engine cost $42,000 (which wouldn't pay for the pump alone, these days).

The American Apparatus pump ran at 1,000 gpm, more than three times the capacity of the '29 and twice that of the '52. On top of the Ford chassis was Albion's first **deluge gun** (also called master stream device, or more graphically, water cannon), which when fed by two 2 ½ inch diameter hoses could throw a heavy stream of water to the upper floors of burning structures. Extra compartment space contained plenty of tools and equipment.

The most controversial aspect of the new pumper had to be its lime green paint job. With the exception of the white rescue squad and the ambulances, all modern AFD trucks had been red. (It's believed the original 1888 engine was black, the color most fire apparatus came in at the time. The hand engines back then often sported ornate decorations, but there's no record of that in Albion. In any case, red became the traditional color about the time motorized fire trucks became popular.)

An optometrist developed lime green to be a "safer" color, more eye catching than red both day and night. By any objective standard, it was unquestionably more visible, even when surrounded by green foliage.

It was also ugly.

Traditionalists argued that red lights and sirens commanded enough attention. It's true few lime green vehicles were on the road, and many red ones; but

The lime green lemon. It probably looks more black and white, to you.

again, detractors pointed out there aren't many trucks out there with emergency lights, sirens, and ladders mounted on them.

When pressed, some firefighters might agree lime green may be the safer color, but still insist a fire truck should be good, old fashioned red. Those who argued that everything possible should be done to keep fire apparatus safe fought a losing battle against traditionalists, who clung to red like a favorite toy.

In the end, the developers of lime green underestimated the power of tradition. Sometimes tradition is bad, such as when firefighters insist on going into hazardous atmospheres without breathing protection. Sometimes it's good, like the tradition of courage and public service that goes with volunteerism.

Tradition also explains why the '29 pumper is still with the AFD, even though the '39 had to be traded in to make room for the trucks that replaced it. No one could stand to part with the department's first gasoline powered engine, which saw 35 years of service and more than its share of fires and parades.

Whichever side of the tradition debate lime green landed on, you don't see it much these days outside of US military bases.

Emergency, Don't Phone Home

As early as January, 1977, some Albionites became interested in the new 911 emergency phone system. But, at a March Town Board meeting, a General Telephone representative said his company couldn't provide the system yet, because the phone company itself wasn't ready for it.

At the same time the Board agreed the firefighters, who by then had all been issued pagers, no longer needed fire phones. The system was removed from individual homes, although the number still ran into the Sheriff's Department and the fire station.

For a few years in the early 80s, the Albion fire number stayed in service after 911 came to town, because after having the old number for so long some people continued to call it. But those times are long gone, and everyone now needs to know the number for 911.

Albion's fire siren remained in service from before the phone to after the pager, and is still used as a tornado siren today. (Still photo from a video courtesy Bill Shultz and the Noble County Historical Society.)

911 is also the place some people call for non-emergencies, but that's a rant for another time.

"A paralyzing snowstorm swept into Noble County last week and held on through the weekend, with mountainous drifts and blowing snow putting almost all traffic to a halt."

So read the *Noble County American's* lead on the worst snowstorm to hit the Midwest in decades. Strong west winds caused whiteout conditions, and 10 foot snow drifts blocked pretty much everything. Few vehicles could move, and most people stayed home – with the exception found in area fire stations.

Although no nearby fires broke out during the worst of the storm, there was plenty for the men to do. Utilizing a dozen snowmobiles and two four wheel drive trucks, they made numerous trips to help stranded people, and manned the station for two and a half days straight.

Three hundred and twelve miles were covered by snowmobiles, and another 100 by four wheel drive. The volunteers delivered groceries, insulin, and other medicines, and checked on families who hadn't been heard from. They brought a pregnant woman into Albion to stay with friends, and made a total of 73 emergency runs during the storm, while being fed themselves by the Red Cross. The storm became a fine example of what fire departments can do besides fighting fires.

School stayed closed for an entire week as crews, using payloaders and dump trucks, carted away piles of snow. It was a long, long week. It's possible even children were ready to go back to school by the time it ended … or maybe not.

As a teen I trekked through chest deep snow to the fire station to see if I could help. There wasn't much for me to do, but it was my first direct contact with volunteer firefighters at work, and left quite an impression on me.

What's on fire?

The idea of a fire in a firehouse leaves room for a lot of jokes. They do happen (fires, not jokes … well, jokes, too.) Fires happen in any place, and although firefighters themselves may crack jokes, they know there's nothing funny about it.

By 1977 several groups, among them Albion's Boxing Club, Park Board, and Boy Scouts, used the fire station basement for activities, and it was being painted in preparation for use as a youth center. On February 18, a Saturday afternoon, "Albion's firemen didn't have far to go to answer the siren", as the *Noble County American* commented.

The blaze started in the furnace room, but didn't spread because of a closed fire door. Chief Applegate speculated the entire station might have been lost, if not for the door.

Fearing the worst, the volunteers braved a fire under their feet and evacuated all the trucks. At the time the '29 was still stored in the southwest corner showroom, and the firefighters found its tires were low and it wouldn't start. Several men worked together to push it out of danger.

Still, for all the excitement, the fire was quickly controlled, especially since firefighters could enter through a side door in the back rather than braving the chimney-like conditions of going down an inside stairwell. Heat caused some damage to the basement roof, but not in an area over which the big trucks parked.

Once the flames were extinguished, a State fire marshal inspected the scene. He declared the blaze wasn't caused by spontaneous combustion, as had been suggested by some who pointed out the rags soaked with paint remover and thinner, along with paint and brushes stored in the furnace room by Park Board workers.

Although he didn't discover the exact cause of the fire, the fire marshal declared it started by *someone* – accidentally or otherwise. Firefighters and Town Board members alike believed it wasn't arson, but never identified the exact cause.

After the furnace was repaired and fire debris cleaned up, the question arose of who should continue to use the basement – if anyone.

The discussion continued over the course of several Town Board meetings. Board member Ted Frymier wanted to know the legalities of groups using the basement, and who would be responsible for future damages. They discussed the possibility of a police officer or firefighter supervising activities, but who would be supervised? The Boy Scouts had adult leaders, but what about dances sponsored by the Park Board, which had been planned for the basement? Supervision wouldn't have prevented the fire anyway, since the basement was unoccupied when the fire broke out.

The Board voted to keep the basement doors locked when not in use, although some wanted to ban its use completely. The fear that another fire might strike the firehouse would prove to be well founded.

Vandalism

Although the basement stayed locked, the upstairs remained unlocked by order of the Town Board. This was, after all, a public building – never mind that the Town Hall was kept locked when unoccupied. The argument went that people reporting emergencies who found no one at the station could run inside, to push the button and set the alert siren off. Sounds reasonable? Sure, as long as no one messes with hundreds of thousands of dollars' worth of emergency equipment, which included portable gear that could be stolen.

Most thieves don't care who they steal from, and several times siphoned gasoline from the truck gas tanks. This conversation took place at an August, 1977, Town Board meeting, as reported in the *Noble County American*:

"'Did you get that pumper fixed?' asked (Town Board member) Knach.

'Yes, it was full of dirt', said (Assistant Chief Joe) Moorhouse. 'We ran out of gas about halfway to Kimmell (on the way to a grain elevator fire). They've been stealing gas out of it again.'"

More problems would come to the station because of the unrealistic notion of keeping it unlocked at all times. Unfortunately, it would be another four years – and two more fires – before the problem would be solved for good.

Insurance Costs

The Insurance Services Office (ISO) is an inspection authority that sets fire protection "averages" for municipalities. If a town improves its fire protection, the number ISO sets for it can get closer to 1, which often lowers insurance rates; if fire protection worsens, the number can approach 10, and bring higher rates for homes, businesses, and industries. Only a few communities, among them Los Angeles, ever get to ISO 1.

In May, 1978, the ISO inspected Albion and pointed out several problems. After the inspection, although one problem with Albion's water pressure and storage system got repaired, the ISO rating rose from 7 to 8, and insurance rates went up.

As Applegate reported to the Town Board, three problems needed correction: a lack of volunteers, replacement of old fire hose, and outdated air packs. Some of the hose had been used only "a dozen times", but was still too old for the ISO, just as a fire pump may still work well but be past its predicted useful age.

The cost to replace hose ran about $14,000, which made the total cost of new equipment $26,000. No one knew where the money would come from, but if improvements were made, Albion could request another inspection.

Three new volunteers joined in May, and the town found the funds to buy new equipment. The episode served to remind Albionites that of the many benefits of a good fire department, some weren't so obvious.

CHAPTER FOURTEEN

One Step Forward
Or,
Two Steps Back

The AFD met the 1980s with several improvements, especially in rural fire protection. It needed a tanker with a larger water capacity, to supplement the one 30-year-old tanker that carried just 1,000 gallons.

What they got was a used fuel tanker: a 1975 Chevy truck that held 2,500 gallons. Unlike the smaller tanker the new unit had its own pump, with which it could fill the dump tank or a pumper, and in an emergency even feed an attack line directly. Instead of the too-small 2 ½-inch dump valve on the old tanker, its large dump valve could empty a load in much less time.

The AFD also needed a new grass truck to replace their

What, lime green? Again? "Tank 1" in front of a 1988 addition to the fire station.

30-year-old government surplus Dodge. Both the grass buggy and the four wheel drive army truck were sold, and the firefighters bought a used 1979 four wheel drive Ford pickup. Like the old trucks, it carried a pump, water tank, hose reel, hand tools, and portable water extinguishers.

The new truck kept its original brown paint job out of a desire to protect its resale value – and was then decaled with the fire department's logo and the designation "Grass 1". There weren't nearly as many complaints about the only known brown fire truck as there were about the '76 engine and the new tanker, both lime green.

Part of that might be because the grass truck proved to be a workhorse. After the volunteers ironed out some early electrical problems, the truck gave

reliable service for over two decades and took everything fires and firefighters could throw at it – which was a lot. More than one firefighter salivated over the idea of having the truck for himself, but when finally retired in 2004, it went to work for Albion's cemetery and continued to chug along in service to the town.

Not lime green lemon, but ... brown beauty? Four wheel Drive for the win.

Eventually it made its way into the hands of that dynasty of Albion firefighting, the Jacob family, and at this writing can be found from time to time at local antique car shows. Although well over thirty years old, it could go right back into action at the next brush fire.

The lime green trucks, on the other hand, well …

The engine ("Pump 3") gave the impression of being thrown together with spare parts, which is possible: The manufacturer hovered close to bankruptcy at the time. It developed continuous problems, and in fact broke down in a cloud of blue smoke on my very first fire call, in July of 1980. More than once it came back to Albion on the tail of a tow truck.

The tanker had more luck, although it also developed occasional electrical problems. Its biggest danger became the brakes, which failed more than once and at the worst moments. This owed to the fact that the repurposed truck was originally designed to carry 2,500 gallons of fuel – which is a great deal lighter than 2,500 gallons of water. In addition, the multiple gears proved to be a nightmare for all but the most experienced drivers, and more than once a firefighter had to push in the clutch, slow to a stop, and start over again from scratch.

It may have been a coincidence, but no Albion fire truck ever saw a lime green paint job again … just in case.

The AFD also put into service a trailer-mounted electrical generator, which could be towed by the grass truck or by any volunteer's vehicle with a trailer hitch. It could turn a nighttime fireground bright as day, but didn't get used often. As technology advanced, the trailer-mounted generator soon became unneeded, since portable generators small enough to fit into a truck's storage compartment became lighter and less expensive.

In early 1981 each of the volunteers received all new turnout gear: helmets, boots, fire resistant pants, and coats. The total cost of outfitting all the firefighters came to $6,000, of which $3,000 came from a Cole Foundation grant, $1,500 from the town budget, and $1,500 was raised by the volunteers themselves. The new gear replaced old rubber coats, helmets that often violated new safety standards, and hip boots that were pulled up like waders. Although some firefighters grumbled about the "Darth Vader" helmet, it made for a drastic improvement in personal safety.

This writer (and you've figured out by now that means me) got impatient and a year earlier purchased the first Darth Vader helmet in the area. To test it, then-Chief Jim Applegate pounded down on it with his fist, as hard as he could - while I was wearing it. I'm happy to report it held up.

Okay, so they were odd looking helmets ... but these guys came home alive.

One of the decade's big changes took place in 1982, when after several years as assistant chief, Larry Huff took over as chief of the AFD. His first year would be a difficult one: Four months after he assumed the post, part of the fire station was again gutted by fire.

Fire Station Burns – Again

At about 10 p.m. on April 24, 1982, someone spotted smoke rising from the roof of the Albion fire station. The first police and fire personnel to arrive, including me (I lived across the street at the time), thought the fire was in a grease rack on the north end.

The grease rack was in an isolated garage area, where vehicles were repaired back when the building was a car dealership. That was directly over where

Firefighters from several departments work to ventilate smoke from the Albion station.

the basement burned five years before, but in this case it turned out the thick black smoke in that area was being generated on the second floor.

This time the antique '29 engine stood safe in Phil Jacob's garage, and remained out of danger. The volunteers drove the other trucks out, laying hose to the nearest hydrants. By the time firefighters headed back in with hose and protective gear the upstairs had "flashed over" – reached the ignition temperature of everything in the room.

Fire engulfed the meeting room, bunk room, and chief's office. Because the upstairs had only one small window, ventilation proved difficult. Firefighters used a power saw, borrowed from the street department, to cut a hole in the roof that would allow smoke

and superheated gasses out. No coincidentally, the firefighters added a power saw to their own inventory soon after.

In addition to twenty Albion firefighters, fire units from Big Lake, Wol Lake, Ligonier, Kendallville, and Rome City came to assist, all traveling a dozen miles or so. Albion's EMS #6, and EMS #2 from Kendallville, treated a number o firefighters for smoke inhalation and heat exhaustion, and transported two of them to the hospital.

The blaze gutted much of the upstairs, destroying records and antique fire equipment. Heat damaged overhead garage doors, while the first floor AFD and Police Department offices suffered heavy smoke and water damage. Albion's base radio and encoder were destroyed; the Rome City Fire Department loaned Albion their old one, to use until a replacement arrived.

The F.A.S.T. arson team from Allen County worked all day Sunday, the day after the fire, to probe the debris. The results were clear: arson. But identifying an arson fire and finding the arsonist are two different tasks, and to this day no arrests have been made in the crime.

That did it for Chief Huff, no matter what Town Board members may have said in the past. The day after the fire he locked the station, to protect the firehouse and the expensive fire equipment housed inside.

Later, after the assessment of several engineers who reacted as if they'd found the place both unsound and radioactive, the AFD moved to its fifth and present station. The aged and damaged former car garage at Orange and Hazel Streets was torn down. It was definitely unsound and contaminated by mold after two major fires and repeated floods in the basement. Radioactive? … Maybe.

In one of those little ironies, the last use of the building was as a practice training ground – for police and firefighters.

Fire Downtown

Like a bookend on a bad year, 1982 closed with another major fire, this one two blocks north of the station. That the cause this time proved accidental – electrical problems – didn't lessen the devastation.

Albion Deputy Marshal Robert Korte drove by on patrol and spotted the fire, on the east side of the courthouse square, and called it in at 12:51 a.m. The first responders to get upstairs saw fire climb a wall in an apartment above Vicki's Fabrics, then spread across the ceiling. Luckily, its occupants were away at the time.

Fire units from Rome City, Kendallville, and Wolf Lake turned out to assist. Firewalls between the apartment and buildings to the north were designed to stop flames from spreading the length of the block, but thick smoke filled the second floor of the *Noble County American* office all the way to the north end of the block, which made it obvious the walls weren't airtight. Firefighters on the roof had to make a trench cut – a hole that extended the entire length of the roof – to stop the fire's spread.

After six hours of hard work, the mutual aid companies left for their home stations, and Albion firefighters took up their hose and prepared to leave the scene. The fire was out – or so they thought.

At 6:34 a.m. Assistant Chief Phil Jacob, who stood with a small group of men at the front (including me; this is the fire that taught me the dangers of overstraining your back), spotted smoke pushing from the roof area at the front. The battle began again.

Rekindles are often worse than the original fire, because the structure has been "opened up" through ventilation and fire damage, which allows fresh air to fan smoldering embers into flames. With plenty of oxygen, the fire will often spread faster even if thousands of gallons of water have already been dumped on it.

So it went this time. By the time firefighters stretched hoselines back upstairs, the entire ceiling area was engulfed, while flames spread into an unoccupied apartment to the south. Intense heat and the danger of collapse drove firefighters out, forcing them into a defensive fire attack. Mutual aid units came in again – more than the first time, from almost every department in the county – and the volunteers used the '76 pumper's deluge gun to throw a stream through second story windows.

Finally, at around 10:30 a.m., exhausted volunteers brought the fire under

Overhaul is sometimes even more manpower intensive than fighting the fire itself, as in this house fire that occupied members of several fire departments.

control again. This time they made *sure* it stayed out. The blaze had spread into a building next door, gutted the upstairs apartments, and did heavy smoke and water damage to Vicki's Fabrics and Gower's Five and Dime Store. Two apartments were damaged beyond repair and torn down, although the first floor of the structure still stands today.

The fire affected other people in unexpected ways. A light breeze to the west sent clouds of smoke toward the Noble County Courthouse, which forced it to close for the day. Officials kept Central Noble High School students, who at the time had an open lunch hour, on campus to cut down on the crowd around the fire scene. Albion Marshall's Posse members, also volunteers, worked through the incident to hold back those crowds and reroute traffic from the downtown area.

It's not uncommon after a fire to hear people complain that the "ax squad" rushed in to tear everything apart even after the fire seemed over, for no good reason – at least, for no good reason anyone can see. It's called overhaul, and the 1982 downtown fire is a perfect example of why it's necessary: to prevent the rekindles that often cause more damage than the original fire.

Fire has a nasty habit of hiding in nooks and crannies as embers that can produce no visible flame or smoke, only to erupt again after firefighters leave the scene. These days thermal imaging cameras help us search for hot spots, but once one is found the ax must come out.

Of course, cameras are an imperfect technology – better than what we had before, but firefighters would rather err on the side of certainty. They don't want to lose what they've already saved once.

One Good Turn ...

As Ligonier responded to Albion's call in 1982, Albion sent a truck to Ligonier for their downtown fire on May 4, 1983 (one day after the 95th anniversary of the AFD's founding). This fire broke out across the alley from the Ligonier fire station, when a torch used in maintenance work set fire to tar on the roof.

In addition to Albion, fire units from Cromwell, Rome City, Kendallville, and Wolf Lake responded, and it took two hours to control the blaze. $75,000 damage resulted to a pharmacy, auto parts store, dentist office, and the Ligonier Eagles Club.

"Jaws of Life"

In 1982 the Noble County government donated sets of Hurst brand extrication tools to several area fire departments, including the AFD. Called "The Jaws of Life" and popularized on the TV show *Emergency!*, the hydraulic tools can pry, cut or lift. Although useful in all sorts of rescues, their main function is to free pinned occupants from car wrecks.

The heavy, unwieldy units have been replaced by lighter designs, but they beat the heck out of hacking away with hand tools. Over the years they proved their worth many times over.

At first the tools went into a compartment the volunteers built on the grass truck. Theoretically, this vehicle could also pump water in case a wrecked car caught fire, or go four-wheel drive for off road rescue situations. But as the rescue squad became better equipped to do the job its name implied, the tools were transferred to it. These days a rescue and an engine are both considered necessary to roll on every personal injury accident.

Albion firefighters hope the owner will never find out they borrowed his car for vehicle extrication training. Albion's third rescue unit, a former beverage delivery truck, is in the background.

1983-4 Calls

The tools gave more evidence that firefighters couldn't just douse flames anymore, and all emergency runs aren't big fires. Other calls in 1983 included an anhydrous ammonia leak on a farm just outside of town, and a call to wash down milk after a semi tanker rolled over while climbing a steep hill on York Street, block from the courthouse. If you don't think a tanker full of spilled milk is a problem, wait until your community is overrun by cats.

The usual rushes came, such as twelve fires in a five day period in March (ten of them grass fires). In a two year period starting in late 1982, five mobile homes burned in the AFD response area: On Albion's south side two children were badly burned while escaping one of those fires.

An incident in 1984 included something most firefighters rarely see – an airplane crash. As two men flew in the small single engine plane, on the lookout for an injured deer, the aircraft lost power and went down. The location couldn't have been much worse: A gully in a rural Green Township woods. The plane wasn't found for hours after it went down.

Dispatchers called the cavalry: ambulances from Albion and Kendallville, State, county, and Albion police, and two fire departments. But uneven ground and heavy underbrush made it difficult to reach the scene, so four wheel drives from Albion and Noble Township, along with more off road vehicles, got people to the scene and evacuated the victims. Tragically, there was one fatality.

Fuel leaked from the plane's wreckage, which hung in the air from trees. Considering the limited amount of fire equipment able to reach the scene, if a fire broke out there wouldn't have been much left.

Still More Water

By now the '52 tanker was over 30 years old, too small, and outdated. It had only one 2 ½ inch diameter dump valve, and no on-board pump. Recognizing their responsibility to a largely rural area, the AFD bought another used fuel tanker, which Captain (and future chief) Bob Beckley spent many hours renovating at his own home.

"New" water tanker, before ...

...And much improved after.

The 1972 Chevy held 2,000 gallons and, like the lime green tanker, came equipped with a dump tank, portable pump, and much larger rear dump valve. It made its first run before it officially went into service, to a grain bin fire north of town in October, 1985. That same fire also proved to be the '52 tanker's last call; it was sold in early 1986 to the town of Rome City. Its ignoble fate: to haul sewage.

With two modernized tankers and help from mutual aid companies, the AFD could now keep up a constant flow of water to most rural fires. Of course, having two tankers also helps maintain coverage when one is called away for mutual aid fires, just as more than one engine keeps the town protected. Water is precious at rural fires, and firefighters depend on neighbors for an extra supply. For instance, an Albion tanker rolled to assist Wolf Lake twice and LaOtto once in December, 1985 alone.

1986: May You Live in Interesting Times

1986 was eventful in more ways than one. Some of the more unusual calls of the year included:

A February accident involved a propane truck that turned over and began leaking at the west junction of SR 9 and US 6, north of Albion. Firefighters called for extra water and applied foam as the truck was uprighted, to reduce the chance of a fire breaking out.

On February 22 only one truck was needed to douse a snowmobile fire, but 15 firefighters showed up when the page went out. As it was the first snowmobile fire in the AFD's recorded history, curiosity might have been a factor in the high turnout.

Later in the year a buildup of paint spray caught fire in a roof vent near the center of a factory, then called P.I.C., in the Albion industrial park. It could have been a disastrous all-day fire, but a single sprinkler head opened up to control the spread of the blaze. Instead of being lost, the building has been expanded and is now part of the Dexter Axle Company.

Three days later, on April 29th, a B&O Railroad car a few miles from Albion developed a sulfuric acid leak. About 300-400 gallons of the liquid, irritating to eyes and skin, spilled. Railroad workers brought five hundred pounds of lime to the scene, to neutralize the acid.

In July the grass truck transported 20 gallons of high expansion foam to Kendallville, where 30 tons of molten metal spilled at Newman Foundry. At that temperature, water sprayed on the metal would cause an explosion, so firefighters used foam to surround it and smother any fire.

On September 14 firefighters' pulses raced at a report of a mobile home fire – with a woman trapped inside. When firefighters arrived they discovered Ruth McGuire and Diane Snyder had already rescued the elderly woman from her Orchard Ridge home, and used a bucket of water to control the flames. The two women were given certificates of honor for their help.

During a heavy snowstorm in November, a Central Noble school bus skidded off the road and overturned, injuring 22 students and the driver. Three fire units joined three ambulances and several police units to treat the injured.

Tire Fire

Despite all that, the most memorable fire of the year – maybe of the decade – took place on March 27. At 1:18 p.m. the Kendallville Fire Department responded to a report of a tire fire at Levin and Sons, Inc. The tires did indeed burn: Tens of thousands of them, piled into mountains dozens of feet high.

Before it ended twenty-three fire departments got involved in the blaze, which threw up a column of black smoke visible from dozens of miles away – according to some reports, hundreds of miles.

The fire turned out to be a bit smaller than the tire fire of '74, which burned in the same location and had even more tires to consume. Details of the two blazes were similar: Both drained Kendallville's water supply, yet neither could be extinguished with water, only contained (with great difficulty). In both cases, bulldozers cut fire breaks and spread dozens of truckloads of sand to stop the blazes, which smoldered for days.

Albion sent the '65 engine and the rescue squad. Nineteen Albion firefighters worked in shifts, totaling 202 man-hours over twelve hours. Naturally, they also took a call to a grass fire in the middle of it all.

On a personal note, in 1974 a friend and I rode in the back of my father's El Camino as we checked out the huge column of smoke, and got tangled up in a traffic jam that almost brought Kendallville to a standstill. I remember an incredible darkness under the shadow of the huge cloud, in my first experience with a major fire.

Twelve years later, I climbed out of my sick bed (while coughing up something really awful) and managed to be on the first Albion truck to head for Kendallville.

In retrospect, both were lamebrain moves.

By the mid 80s the AFD found itself in a position somewhat the opposite of the problem faced 50 years before. In the 30s the AFD stood prepared for fires in town, but rural responses were crippled by a lack of water. Fifty years later they had two tankers, a shuttle system that employed dump tanks and large diameter valves, and a habit of calling for mutual aid much more quickly. Now city protection became the challenge.

New and larger buildings went up, but size wasn't the main problem. Modern construction materials are more lightweight. Once fire breaks out, they tend to burn more quickly, and at higher temperatures. To make matters worse, the '76 engine kept experiencing mechanical problems, and more than one volunteer questioned how much it could be trusted.

Another '65, showing off at another Chain O' Lakes Festival parade ... sometimes older is better.

With the '52 aging, and its pump capacity only 500 gpm (excellent in 1952; lousy in 1986), the Insurance Services Organization would likely refuse to consider it as proper fire protection on their next inspection, which would once again lead to higher insurance rates. A new fire engine was needed.

To some people, the obvious isn't always so obvious. Trustees of the townships protected by the AFD had to agree on a new purchase; some of the trustees and their advisory board members opposed it, apparently because it involved spending money. That effectively blocked any purchase from the AFD budget, and money available elsewhere was limited.

The volunteers scraped together enough funds for the next best thing, a *used* fire engine, which in the interest of political correctness I suppose should be called pre-owned. They couldn't wait any longer: Because of breakdowns of the '76, the 36 year old '52 answered several calls in 1986.

(Volunteers have a long tradition of scraping money together through various fundraisers, such as the AFD's annual fish fry, and other imaginative techniques such as begging local businesses. Profits for the book you're holding in your hand go to the department, so stop browsing and pony up.)

The Ligonier Fire Department sold Albion their 1965 unit for $17,000. Like the '76, it was built by the American Fire Apparatus company, but it was made ten years before that company faced financial troubles – which made all the difference.

In addition to being 13 years newer, it pumped twice as much water as the '52 – 1,000 gpm. The biggest difference, though, was the older truck's design as a rural firefighting unit, compared to the newer one's layout for city use.

The new '65 combined a pumper and city service truck, which is a unit designed to carry out the operations of a ladder truck when a ladder truck isn't close by. It carried only 260 gallons of on-board water, but a pre-piped deluge gun on top could be put into operation immediately on big fires.

The pump was also unusual. All other Albion engines had two-stage pumps, but this one had four stages. It was designed to pump water out of the Elkhart River, or over long distances in case of a water shortage in Ligonier. It could pump 1,000 gpm at 250 pounds of pressure per square inch; but, if the operator needed pressure to make up for a long run of hose, it could be changed from "series" to "parallel" and pump 250 gpm – at *1,000* psi. Try holding onto *that* hoseline.

The smaller water tank made room for two extra ladders beyond the 35 footers mounted on the other engines: One a 24 foot extension ladder that in a pinch could be raised by one firefighter, and the other a 45 foot Bangor ladder.

There are a few buildings in town beyond the reach of a 35 foot ladder – one of them is the courthouse, of course. The volunteers were a bit intimidated by the Bangor ladder (It was invented in Bangor, Maine), which required five men to raise and was so tall poles could be attached to the side for added stability.

There was also room on the engine for more ventilation and

Albion received its first deluge gun (technically called a master stream device) in 1976. Modern deluge guns can deliver the full capacity of the fire pump.

overhaul tools, making this the closest thing to a ladder truck in Albion since the original hook and ladder wagon.

More Modern Equipment

The old rescue squad began to develop its share of mechanical problems, and ran out of space as more rescue and fire support equipment came on line. Plus, it was too darned top heavy. In late 1986 a 1983 Utility-Master van came along, with more room and a bit more stability.

The volunteers renovated the vehicle, and organized it for as much equipment as possible. It now held not only the Hurst extrication tools, but also a power generator, extension cords and flood lights, a foam generator and containers of high expansion foam, two power saws, SCBA and extra air tanks, smoke ejecting fans, portable oxygen, and first aid supplies.

Albion's fire rescue unit – which didn't even exist 20 years before – made more responses in 1987 than any other fire truck on the department. To this day, the rescue rolls on every accident and most fire calls. Now, with the equipment transferred to the AFD's fourth rescue vehicle, it remains one of the department's most important pieces of equipment.

Firefighters and medics train for hazardous materials incidents along the railroad tracks near Albion, in the late 80s. On the right is the author, in one of the few times he's been pictured actually doing something. Which, come to think of it, isn't complimentary. (Photo courtesy Albion Fire Department)

CHAPTER FIFTEEN

The Albion Fire Department Today
Or,
(By which I mean 25 years ago.)

This brings us to 1988 – a century in the future, for those intrepid townspeople who tackled the fire fiend to keep their community alive. Albion's "fire heroes" continue to answer the call, and with the addition of so many new services the number of calls is sure to continue increasing.

Firefighters never know what their next challenge will be. In March of 1987, they battled 8 fires in one day, but a call could just as easily be for a chemical spill, a heart attack, or someone pinned in the wreckage of their car. A sample from '87:

In April an ammonia leak forced the evacuation of the Noble County Courthouse's first floor.

In May several trucks helped the Noble Township Fire Department battle a feed mill fire in Wolf Lake.

In July a semi hit a bull when it wandered onto SR 9, south of Albion, unleashing a chain reaction of challenges. The impact forced the semi into a culvert, and caused damage that dumped 100 gallons of diesel fuel into a stream. Firefighters had to construct a dike to prevent contamination, place ladders across the stream to reach the truck cab and help remove the driver's body, get into the truck's load to make sure it wasn't hazardous, set up foam lines in case of a fire, and illuminate the investigation scene. All in one call.

In August, an AFD engine and the rescue truck headed into a traffic-jammed Kendallville when fire broke out at Val's Discount Store on a busy Friday night.

On Halloween night, Rome City and Noble Township firefighters helped for three hours at a house fire just outside of Albion. I went along – dressed as Groucho Marx under my turnout gear.

AFD members came out to ventilate when torches being used by construction workers spread smoke into the Noble County Jail.

Boat fires are unusual, even with all the lakes in the area, but 1987 saw one near Summit Lake. The irony is that firefighters found the boat engulfed in flames – while on a trailer parked along the roadway.

That's just a sample, of course. If there's one thing firefighters have learned, it's that they must assume a worst case scenario with each and every call, until they arrive at the scene and know for sure. Sometimes a fire is knocked down before they arrive, or a person reported trapped in wreckage walks away from an accident, but they must respond with everything they might need.

Fire Calls

In the late 80s, before the number of runs swelled as the AFD implemented medical assist calls, the AFD averaged 75-80 runs per year. Naturally, the number varies – the weather can make a big difference in, for instance, car accidents and grass fires, and no one can predict how many structure fires will break out.

An old tradition has it that calls always come in threes; true or not, they do happen in bunches. At a time when the AFD averaged a call every four days, the volunteers got called out more than once a day 29 times from 1984-1987, and more than twice a day 6 times. On seven occasions the firefighters hustled to answer more than one call at the same time. That's not likely to change.

Resources in 1988

In 1988 the AFD had 27 volunteers, commanded by Chief Larry Huff, Assistant Chief Phil Jacob, and Captains Bob Beckley, Kevin Libben, and Steve Caswell. Under an ongoing training program, almost all the volunteers became state-certified firefighters, with the rookies required to meet that goal within two years of joining. Several had master firefighter certifications, although changes in state training guidelines made some of the old certifications questionable later on – not because there was anything wrong with the training, but because the older certifications didn't fit in with the state's new rules.

Like most volunteer fire departments, the amount of manpower available to the AFD drops on weekdays, when members have jobs they can't leave, or work out of town. That's become more of a problem as time goes by, and departments depend on help from neighboring fire departments.

Protective firefighting clothing changed in the 80s. By 1988, instead of a rubber coat and thigh length boots, the ensemble included coats, pants, and hoods made of high tech material, in addition to the boots and gloves. The "Darth Vader" style helmets became less popular as time went by, mostly because they just didn't look by-gosh traditional enough. By the turn of the century they'd been mostly replaced by more traditional looking helmets with an advanced design.

Those awful steel air tanks, which were responsible for a 1983 injury that left me with chronic back pain, also started going away, replaced by much lighter and more comfortable metal-fiberglass hybrids. Once the face mask goes on, a modern firefighter is completely encapsulated.

Unfortunately, this protective shield lessens their ability to feel changes in the atmosphere around them, so firefighters must now be better trained to read smoke and fire conditions in order to avoid getting caught too far in when things go bad.

Smoke inhalation is much less of a danger now, but heat exhaustion is a different story. Fighting fire in winter? The encased firefighter, as he works with heavy equipment, still gets worn down by stress and exertion. Bystanders who make jokes about

Firefighters rehab -- rest and rehabilitate -- at a fire near downtown. Behind them is Albion's newest rescue truck, and behind it the Noble County Historical Society Old Jail Museum -- which happens to be where Albion's early 1900s hose cart is. It's the circle of firefighting life.

firefighters standing around don't realize those men and women just finished work equivalent to running a marathon – or they're waiting to replace other teams as they do that work – or they're on standby in case they need to rescue a fallen comrade.

Looking back, I've realized almost all the equipment we had in-service in 1988 is gone now – which makes sense, since that was 25 years ago and depending on old emergency equipment is a bad idea. The grass truck, now privately owned, is going strong in retirement. The '75 and '72 tankers and the original rescue van are all gone, after responding to just about every rural fire and many in town. The second rescue truck is now in use by the Town of Albion Utilities Department.

In mid-1988 – a year full of big changes – the '52 fire engine was auctioned off. Some of the firefighters (including me) would have liked to keep it as an antique, as they did the '29, but money and space had to be reserved for newer equipment.

Tired of increasingly expensive repair bills, the firefighters sold the '76 engine the same year, and put the money toward the purchase of a new truck. At the time they thought another engine would arrive soon to replace it, but, as with the '76, legal and paperwork problems delayed the new truck by several months.

That left the AFD, at the time the first draft of this book was written, with just two engines: The '65 Chevy and the '65 Ford. (I'll let you Chevy and Ford purists fight it out amongst yourselves.) But as I said, 1988 became a year of big changes, and before the year was out Pump 91 – a 1988 International with a 1,000 gpm pump and 1,500 gallon water tank – came on line.

Here stood a truck designed for rural service, with three times the on-board water as any previous Albion engine – in fact, it could technically be called a pumper-tanker. That

This 1988 International fire engine was the next generation -- until the next generation came along. That UFO in the background is Albion's second water tower.

made it ideal for fast attacks on any structure fire, rural or town, and as larger tanker trucks were placed into service the call of "more water!" became much less common.

But time passes, and in May, 2012, the 1988 truck was replaced by a new engine. Our 25 year workhorse was sent to a small fire department in Kentucky, and now proudly serves that community.

In response to bigger trucks in the aging fire station, in early 1988 (I *told* you it was a big year), the firefighters built an addition to the east side of the fire station, which provided enough room to park two more trucks. But the place stayed crowded – and old. On a scarier note, structural engineers instructed the firefighters never to back two trucks in at the same time, out of fear that the apparatus bay of the former auto dealership would collapse into the basement.

There was a problem. That, and the ongoing space crunch, led to a new station on the east side of Albion, which went up in 1997.

It was Albion's fifth firehouse in 110 years, since A.J. Denlar took command of his three hand-drawn apparatus. That's a good place to end our story, although of course, the story of the Albion Fire Department goes on.

Farewell, see you in 2038

Why haven't I covered the intervening 25 years in this volume, the time between 1988 and, as I write this, 2013?

Well, because I'm tired.

Also because I've hit 46,000 words, which when combined with photos is a fair-sized book already. Covering a hundred years of history isn't a sprint, it's a marathon.

In addition, it occurs to me that – don't laugh at this – someone might want to put out a new addition for the 150th anniversary of the AFD. After all, that's 25 years away, and surely some future historian will be happy to cover the end of the 20th Century.

And, finally, I've considered the idea of something a bit more autobiographical, to cover my thirty years on the line from a personal standpoint. If there's enough interest, maybe in a few years I'll write the AFD's more recent history the way I lived it. I'll be famous by then. Of course, I when I was eighteen I said I'd be famous by *now*.

Things change. At this writing the 1988 engine is newly retired, and one of the two tankers qualifies as a pumper itself. The rescue truck, rather than a former bread or soda delivery vehicle, is designed for rescue services, and water rescue equipment has been added to the inventory. Instead of one grass truck, the AFD now has two – which do double duty as medical assist first responder vehicles.

The Albion Fire Department will continue to advance in training and technology, to better battle the "fire fiend" in the future. Whatever happens, you can be sure there'll be adventures to come, new stories to tell, and plenty of challenges.

APPENDIX

Albion Fire Chiefs

1887-1888	A.J. Denlar
1888-1893	?
1894	William E. Worden
1895-1897	?
1898	George O. Russell Jr.
1899-1924	?
1925-1930	John Gatwood
1930-1937	?
1937-1952	Harry Campbell
1952-1954	Byron K. Smith
1954-1959	Harry Metz
1959-1963	Robert Beckley
1963-1969	Al Jacob
1970-1971	James Applegate
1971-1973	Edward Moorhouse
1974-1975	Terry Campbell
1975-1981	James Applegate
1982-1993	Larry Huff
1994-1997	Bob Beckley

1998-2001	Kevin Libben
2002-2008	Gregg Gorsuch
2009-2010	Brad Rollins
2011-2012	Tim Lock
2013	Steve Bushong

Membership of the Albion Fire Department just after the department's 100th anniversary.

Membership of the Albion Fire Dept. on May 4, 1988:

Chief Larry Huff
Asst. Chief Phil Jacob
Captain Bob Beckley
Captain Kevin Libben
Captain Steve Caswell
Secretary Tim Lock
Treasurer Mitch Fiandt

Dan Anderson
Rick Anderson
Wayne Baker
Roger Boggs
Jim Bortner
Mike Campbell
Terry Campbell
Ron Coats
Gregg Gorsuch
Roy Hendricks
Mark R. Hunter
Denny Kirkpatrick
Steve Kirkpatrick
Tom Lock
Joe Moorhouse
Mark Pulver
Rex Rossman
Duane Simpson
Ray Dean Snyder
Gary Weeks

Additional Photos

A hose crew moves in on the Camp Lutherhaven fire.

More "Darth Vader" helmets in action; at the bottom right a firefighter wears an even older style helmet.

Albion's newest tanker also qualifies as an engine... and flies a cool flag in this parade.

A look from inside the burned out- building at the first Albion fire engine to have a top-mounted pump control panel, which is safer and more visible for the operator.

AFD firefighters do a ceremonial (and practical) wash down of the just-delivered '96 rescue truck.

The AFD in 1988 in its auto dealership-turned fire station. Visible trucks and their ages: Grass 1 (1979), Rescue 1 (1983), Pump 4 (1965), and Tank 2 (1972).

Run Reports

Movies, TV shows, the evening news – that's where you see all the fun stuff. Never mind that the action shots mean someone's lost their home, livelihood, or life – it's still gripping, dramatic stuff. Would the TV show *Emergency!* ever have been made without the exclamation point? In other words, would anyone want to watch Johnny Gage and Roy DeSoto restock their drug box, test their equipment, wash the truck, and fill out run reports?

Ah, run reports. As the old joke goes, the job's never over until the paperwork's done. (And if you've never heard the old joke, imagine that line along with a roll of toilet paper.)

For fans of history and statistics, paperwork is a treasure trove that would startle and bemuse the people who filled it out at the time. You can learn a lot by putting the numbers together, although in the end the numbers on the Albion Fire Department's run reports show a predictable trend: Firefighters get busier, and their job more complicated.

I dug through musty, dusty, and smoke stained boxes that survived two fire station fires, and found run reports covering almost all of two periods: 1956-59, and 1982-87. Surely there are more records around somewhere, but the dust allergies got to me.

Again, the three big things I learned are givens to anyone in the business:

1. The business is unpredictable.

For instance, in March of 1957 the AFD answered 10 calls, but in June they had a run-free month. In 1962 they had one of those fun-filled dry springs that led to 15 calls in March. In August, the month after my birth, none at all. (A heat wave struck that year, so they were probably grateful.)

Similarly, while the total number of runs continued to rise as time went by, some years got a lot busier than others for various reasons (see below about weather). 1966 bottomed out at 36 runs, three years after the volunteers faced their busiest wildland fire season in ten years.

It would be cost effective to cut a fire department's inventory by 75% or so, then go rent equipment and train manpower in advance of a drought, busy spell, or disaster. Cost effective, but impossible to predict what may be needed when.

2. The weather is just as unpredictable.

During the period surveyed, March experienced by far the busiest month, averaging eight calls, with September as the slowest. At the time the busiest month for grass, brush, and field fires was March, although that's now migrated for whatever reason to April.

And yet, in 1960 the AFD didn't get a single call in March, and in 1959, instead of being the slowest month, September became the second busiest.

Wildland fires aren't the only type of calls affected by the weather. If there's a rash of vehicle accidents, such as in 1986 and 1987, you can be sure we had a bad winter. The same thing goes if the number of chimney fires increases, although that number also fluctuates with the economy and the cost of fuel.

3. There's always something new.

When Albion firefighters answered 27 calls in 1960 they weren't trained as first responders, didn't have the tools to handle vehicle extrication, and never even

heard the term hazardous materials. In 1969, the volunteers ran an ambulance service and hit the triple digits with 113 calls, 49 of them medical related. After not one recorded vehicle accident through the 60s, in 1986 the AFD ran on 18 of them. The average number of weather watches, standbys, fuel leaks, and hazardous material calls tripled over the years, although major HazMat incidents remain few.

Cold water rescue drills in a driving snowstorm. Who would have thought, back in 1888, that the AFD would one day have an entire complement of water and ice rescue equipment?

I'm presenting – if all goes well with the printer – the tables of run reports for those two periods. Everyone loves numbers, right? I might take an algebra class, just for fun. The numbers pretty much speak for themselves, and if there's a fluctuation from year to year the weather and economy are usually accountable.

I have no explanation for why, in 1983, I found 15 run reports that didn't specify any type. Considering a series of major snowstorms swept through the area that year, I'd bet they were weather related. That's the way it goes when you deal with old records – although, considering I was on as a three year rookie then, it doesn't seem so very old to me.

Year	1956	1957	1958	1959	1960	1961	1962
Business/Public	1	1	1	0	2	2	1
Home	3	4	3	0	5	5	7
Barn	1	4	2	3	2	1	2
M.Home	0	0	0	1	0	0	0
Shed/Garage	1	1	0	2	1	0	2
Chimney	1	1	2	1	0	4	1
Grass/Brush/Field	11	12	7	8	6	2	18
Vehicle	4	6	4	3	3	1	2
False Alarm	2	0	1	4	1	0	0
Minor/Other fire	11	9	8	10	6	14	8
Haz Mat/Fuel	0	0	0	1	1	2	0
Weather/Standby	0	0	0	0	0	0	0
Accident	0	0	0	0	0	0	0
EMS	0	0	0	0	0	0	0
Total	35	38	28	33	27	31	41

Year	1963	1964	1965	1966	1967	1968	1969
Business/Public	1	0	0	0	0	1	1
Home	5	2	7	5	3	2	4
Barn	3	2	3	3	2	3	3
M.Home	1	1	2	0	2	1	0
Shed/Garage	3	1	0	0	1	1	5
Chimney	0	0	1	0	3	3	0
Grass/Brush/Field	23	22	12	12	3	12	26
Vehicle	7	6	5	5	3	5	5
False Alarm	0	0	1	0	0	3	6
Minor/Other fire	9	8	10	3	9	7	9
Haz Mat/Fuel	0	1	0	0	1	1	2
Weather/Standby	0	0	0	0	3	1	3
Accident	0	0	0	0	0	0	0
EMS	0	0	3	8	20	36	49
Total	52	43	44	36	50	76	113

Year	1982	1983	1984	1985	1986	1987
Business/Public	2	2	0	0	4	3
Home	2	5	5	9	3	7
Barn	1	1	3	5	4	3
Mobile Home	2	2	1	1	1	1
Shed/Garage	0	3	2	2	3	3
Chimney	3	4	1	4	9	3
Grass/Brush/Field	10	18	20	9	5	18
Vehicle	5	8	9	8	11	1
False Alarm	2	3	1	3	7	4
Minor Fire/Other	7	5	6	14	9	6
Haz Mat/Fuel Leak	1	1	1	2	4	3
Weather/Standby	5	2	0	4	6	2
Vehicle Accident	6	2	4	8	18	19
EMS assist	3	1	0	3	1	1
Unspecified	0	15	0	0	0	0
Total	49	72	53	72	85	74

Made in the USA
Lexington, KY
28 June 2013